"When our heart is filled with love, our act a freedom that fosters deep connections wi statement beautifully expresses the wisdom of Islene Runningdeer's book, *Musical Encounters with Dying: Stories and Lessons*. The book shows the power of love, of connection, of understanding, along with musical skill, that brings to the dying the truth that 'music can feed the hungry soul'. At the end of the book, Islene's gift to us is her song, 'May Your Soul Be Well'. Her work has enabled many to find the wisdom of their souls."

—*Ferris Buck Urbanowski, MA, Senior Instructor, Co-ordinator of Professional Training, Currently Adjunct Faculty, The Center for Mindfulness, University of Massachusetts Medical Center, Emeritus Faculty, Departments of Applied Psychology and Environmental Studies, Antioch New England, Honorary Lecturer, University of Wales, Bangor, Wales*

"Islene Runningdeer is an artist in sound. Her experiences of ministering to the dying (and the people who love them) through music and song are beautifully rendered here in the stories of Agnus, Kathy, Winifred, Ethan, and many other memorable souls who belong to her colorful, crusty, welcoming, challenging community. This is a book for aspiring music therapists, hospice teams, caregivers, and anyone who will someday face death. Oh…that's all of us, isn't it? Then let us all read this work of this wise musician, an experienced caregiver herself, and let us all sing the praises of these stories of our parents, sisters, brothers, neighbors, and friends, and how they were touched by compassionate care, and music."

—*Jonna Goulding, MD, Hospice and Palliative Medicine Specialist*

"We can explore with this book what we might want our own end to be. Islene leads us with heartfelt story and song on the intimacies of the last adventure. When we travel to places we don't know, we use a guide book. Islene gives us one, the music book of stories we have stored in our hearts. From lullabies and rock and roll, to sounds of pageantry, dance tunes, and ecclesiastical soaring, she shows how the ending melts into the music of the spheres, guiding our way home."

—*Kathy Panagiotes, MA, MSN, RN, Professor and Program Chair, Mt. Wachusett Community College*

of related interest

Comforting Touch in Dementia and End of Life Care
Take My Hand
Barbara Goldschmidt and Niamh van Meines
Illustrated by James Goldschmidt
Published by Singing Dragon
ISBN 978 1 84819 073 3
eISBN 978 0 85701 048 3

The Creative Arts in Palliative Care
Edited by Nigel Hartley and Malcolm Payne
ISBN 978 1 84310 591 6
eISBN 978 1 84642 802 9

Dying, Bereavement and the Healing Arts
Edited by Gillie Bolton
Foreword by Baroness Professor Ilora Finlay of Llandaff
ISBN 978 1 84310 516 9
eISBN 978 1 84642 680 3

Making Sense of Near-Death Experiences
A Handbook for Clinicians
Edited by Mahendra Perera, Karuppiah Jagadheesan and Anthony Peake
Foreword by Janice Holden
ISBN 978 1 84905 149 1
eISBN 978 0 85700 342 3

Communicating with Children
When a Parent is at the End of Life
Rachel Fearnley
ISBN 978 1 84905 234 4
eISBN 978 0 85700 475 8

Palliative Care, Ageing and Spirituality
A Guide for Older People, Carers and Families
Elizabeth MacKinlay
ISBN 978 1 84905 290 0
eISBN 978 0 85700 598 4

Musical Encounters with Dying

Stories and Lessons

Islene Runningdeer

Foreword by Diana Peirce

Jessica Kingsley *Publishers*
London and Philadelphia

Consent has been given for all case study material and pseudonyms have been used. Photograph on p.5 copyright © Lindsey Vladyka 2013, reproduced with kind permission from the photographer. "The Silver Swan" lyrics by Orlando Gibbons on p.21 are reproduced with kind permission from E.C. Schirmer Music Company. Copyright © 1936, 1964 by E.C. Schirmer Music Company, a division of ECS Publishing, www.ecspub.com. Used By Permission. The "You Are My Sunshine" lyrics by Jimmie Davis on p.22 are reproduced with kind permission from Peer International Corporation. Copyright © 1940 by Peer International Corporation. Copyright Renewed. Used by Permission. "The Lost Cord" lyrics by Arthur Sullivan on p.33 are reproduced with kind permission from Novello & Co. Copyright © Novello & Co. Ltd. International Copyright Secured. All Rights Reserved. Used by Permission. "The Art Spirit" excerpt by Robert Henri on p.91 is reproduced with kind permission from HarperCollins Publishers. Copyright 1923 J.B. Lippincott Company. Copyright renewed 1951 by Violet Organ. Introduction copyright 1930 by J.B. Lippincott Company. Copyright renewed 1958 by Forbes Watson. Reprinted by permission of HarperCollins Publishers. "The Soul's Code" excerpt by James Hillman on p.105 is reproduced with kind permission from Grand Central Publishing. The "Distressed Haiku" from *The Painted Bed* by Donald Hall on p.120 is reproduced with kind permission from Houghton Mifflin. Copyright © 2002 by Donald Hall. Reprinted by permission of Houghton Mifflin Harcourt Publishing Company. All rights reserved. The "Love Poems from God" excerpt by Meister Eckhart on p.125 is reproduced with kind permission from Penguin Group Publishing. The "Alice Blue Gown" lyrics by Joseph McCarthy on p.130 are reproduced with kind permission from Alfred Music Publishing Co. Copyright © 1919 (Renewed) EMI Feist Catalog Inc. All Rights Controlled by EMI Feist Catalog Inc. (Publishing) and Alfred Publishing Co., Inc. (Print). All Rights Reserved. Used by Permission. The "Gravity and Grace" excerpt by Simone Weil (1952, p.178) on p.135 is reproduced with kind permission from Taylor and Francis.

First published in 2013
by Jessica Kingsley Publishers
116 Pentonville Road
London N1 9JB, UK
and
400 Market Street, Suite 400
Philadelphia, PA 19106, USA

www.jkp.com

Copyright © Islene Runningdeer 2013
Foreword copyright © Diana Peirce 2013
Author photograph copyright © Duback Photography 2013

Library of Congress Cataloging in Publication Data
Runningdeer, Islene.
Musical encounters with the dying : stories and lessons / Islene Runningdeer ; foreword by Diana Peirce.
pages cm
Includes bibliographical references and index.
ISBN 978-1-84905-936-7 (alk. paper)
1. Music thanatology. I. Title.
ML3920.R86 2013
615.8'5154--dc23
2012051532

British Library Cataloguing in Publication Data
A CIP catalogue record for this book is available from the British Library

ISBN 978 1 84905 936 7
eISBN 978 0 85700 748 3

Printed and bound in Great Britain

For all the soloists
who have taken
their final bows

and

for my mother,
Doris Marie Leger Progen
(1926–2011)

Contents

Foreword

It was in the late fall of 2000 in Vermont, a time of preparation for what is to come. For most of us, it is preparation for the long, cold winter ahead. For some of us, it is for letting go, the end of life. Islene Runningdeer was known to me as the private caregiver of a recently deceased hospice patient who had been in our care. When she approached me about introducing music therapy to our Hospice and Palliative Care program, I was interested. Long a believer in the value of the integrative therapies, I knew that music would add much to our patients' lives. However, our program was small and our budget tight. I suggested that she could be the one to secure grant funding for a short pilot. Following this, we would consider the feasibility of offering the service. Islene successfully secured a grant, and in mid-2001, she joined our group.

On these pages, Islene chronicles but a few of the lives we shared in caring for during our ten years together. As I read, their faces and many others came to mind. Experiences of living—really living—even as life ebbed. The small fingers of a seven-year-old playing melodies on a harp; hands gnarled by age and circumstance, tapping in time to some long ago tune; anxiety, anger and pain eased as hearts and minds are transported to easier, safer times.

However, what is missing from this book and what was an unanticipated but treasured benefit from adding music therapy (and this music therapist) to our team was, and is, the lasting effect on staff and the many ways we learned to minister to one another through this medium.

2001 proved to be a year of uncertainty and tragedy throughout our nation (America) and our world, as well as in our rural Hospice and Palliative Care team, but for different reasons. Soon after Islene joined us, tragedy visited our group when a beloved nurse team member died unexpectedly. He was a musician who shared his gift with both colleagues and patients. As we tried to find our way through this dense sadness, Islene helped us to fill some of the void. In all, three staff members died (including one who was actually in our care during her ten years with the team). We worked together to memorialize, honor, and bid farewell to each of these, our beloved friends, in music and song.

There were community memorial services twice each year for which Islene played and organized the musical offerings—always just right for the 200-plus family, friends, and colleagues in attendance.

Then there were the fun times—our deep voiced music therapist bouncing a tambourine on her hip as she and our intern taught us words they'd written and set to a familiar tune to help nurses remember some new regulatory requirements. We prepared for our part in organizational special events—always together, always in song.

My point is that music therapy added to the strength that held us together. It wasn't the only thing, but it certainly played an important role and enhanced our capacity to provide one another— colleagues, friends, patients, families—with the best possible care, and encouraging each to live, and live fully, even as they died.

I am honored to add my voice to the chorus of appreciation for music as an end of life care necessity, and to Islene Runningdeer for patiently teaching me its value.

Diana Peirce, RN, CHPN
The Elizabeth Hospice
San Diego, California
Former Director of Hospice and Palliative Care
Central Vermont Home Health and Hospice
Barre, Vermont

Acknowledgments

I've crossed paths with many fine, knowledgeable and even wise people in my life. I've also run into more than a few scoundrels, but even these encounters have taught me some important things. I hope you know who you are, because I can't list all of you here.

The people I wish to specifically acknowledge are the members of a top-notch hospice team in Central Vermont which served Washington and Orange Counties between the years 2001 and 2011. Under the inspired and indefatigable direction of Diana Peirce, RN, who devoted 30 years of her career to the development and guidance of hospice care in rural communities, a very special group of nurses, aides, social workers, therapists and volunteers came together during that decade to provide some of the best end of life care available in this country. The work we did surpassed the norm because we knew how important it was to work as a team, to communicate freely and often with each other, to keep learning new things, to laugh and cry together, to take care of ourselves and each other, and to give the highest priority to the needs of our patients and families. Some of you were longtime veterans of 10, 20 years or more. Some of you were younger, not long out of nursing school. Members of this stellar, core group know who you are, I trust. I thank and love you all for teaching me, for supporting me in my work.

And to the brightest love-lights of my life, I give great thanks to my daughter Tawnya Kristen and granddaughter Olivia True. My dear girls.

Notes on the text

The names of all characters in these stories, with the exception of my mother's, have been changed to honor their privacy. All the events in the stories are true.

Preface

For ten years, between 2001 and 2011, I worked on a rural hospice team in Central Vermont, providing therapeutic musical experiences to dying patients and their families. Throughout my 64 years on this planet, music has followed me, as I have followed it. Landing a position on a well-respected clinical team of nurses, aides, social workers, and other therapists at mid-life was a welcomed result of many years of musical work and study; performing, educating, and developing a growing understanding of how music affects us, how a deep relationship with music can heal us. I finally had an opportunity to practice music as service to others, something that felt just right to me. Being of service to those who are terminally ill, and the people around them who are anticipating a big loss, was an answer to a calling. I believed very deeply, given my own personal experiences with the power of music, that this could be a way to shine light and joy and calm on a transition that too many in our culture fear and try to ignore. Death will visit us all, after all. So, I thought, shouldn't we do what we can to "make friends" with it? I believed that, using music as an expressive and convincing language, I might be able to help people shake hands with death and move forward with grace, acceptance and ease. A decade of work proved that I was right.

Central Vermont is a very beautiful region of mountains, valleys and rivers, punctuated by quaint villages, hardscrabble towns, an aging working-class city that supplies granite to the rest of the world and our colorful and quirky state capital. My hospice team provided home-based care, so I traveled many a rugged road in my all-wheel-drive vehicle, packed with an assortment of instruments and music, in every kind of weather. People of all persuasions populate this landscape: aging descendants of European immigrants who worked the granite quarries, educated folks who carry on state government, prolific artists of all types, hard-working farmers managing to keep alive an old agricultural tradition, back-to-the-land hippies who stayed beyond the 1970s to see this state grow into a little powerhouse of progressive politics, and then, of course, the very rich and the very poor. Death spares none of us, so I managed to meet a variety of people from each of these diverse worlds. Music was a language we all understood on some level and it helped me to build warm, supportive relationships with many people, some very different from myself, who had little time to waste. It provided a small patch of common ground upon which we could stand (or sit, or lie down) together, and begin the hard work of facing the most difficult thing: end of life.

People in hospice care generally have foreknowledge of their impending deaths. This brings with it both great challenges and opportunities. The difficult emotions of fear, regret, anger, sadness are often counterbalanced by an urge to do final things: to take on a last work project, to re-experience the romance of a long-time marriage, to explore unresolved spiritual questions, to find a way to thank people for a lifetime of friendship, to revisit childhood memories, to put away anger and resistance and finally accept loving care, to find meaning and value at a time of life when everything must become simple, to mend bad relations or to accept the impossibility of doing so, to make and sing one's own death song.

I have been witness to the valiant efforts of the dying to accomplish such lofty things in their final weeks and days. But I have also been their accompanist in these endeavors. Accompanying soloists, singers and instrumentalists, has been a favorite personal musical experience of mine for many years. I came to understand while working with the dying that that, indeed, was my role in the life-music we were making together. A good accompanist is always listening to the soloist, always supporting and adding something beautiful and creative to enhance the solo line. She is prepared for surprises, mishaps, the necessity to make sudden adjustments, as well as staying open to enjoying the wondrous musical moments that two people can make and share together. It's a lovely piece of teamwork. But the spotlight is always on the soloist, in this case, the one who is preparing to die.

I'd like to share with my readers some of the stories and lessons that grew out of these special opportunities for deep relationship. When I embarked on this journey in 2001, I hoped and trusted that the musical experience, in the hands of a sensitive and caring therapist, could be an effective way to help people walk down the final trail. As I write this, more than ten years later, I couldn't be more convinced and satisfied that this is indeed true.

One

The Death Song
Historical and Therapeutic Perspectives

"The silver swan, who living had no note,
When death approached, unlocked her silent throat.
Leaning her breast against the reedy shore,
Thus sang her first and last, and sang no more."

Five-part Madrigal for Mixed Voices,
Orlando Gibbons, 1583–1625

Mavis was an elderly woman living out her final months with family friends of meager means. Mavis's face was deeply lined, mapping the many struggles and losses of her long life. Of her eight children, six had already predeceased her, some in tragic circumstances. I was always surprised to find her in agreeable and friendly spirit, despite all that she had endured.

I sat with her many times before her death, singing and talking and listening to her stories. Each session had to include the singing of "You Are My Sunshine," Mavis's favorite song of all. Written in 1939, it must have been number one on the charts during the youth of many elder hospice patients, so often do they request it, but for Mavis I think it meant something very special. Whenever I sang it to her, or we sang it together, we would look deeply into each other's eyes without self-consciousness. And in that moment, I imagined her remembering each of her departed children, as she herself was preparing to die. As old as she was, she took on the look of an innocent child as she sang: "You'll never know, dear, how much I love you. Please don't take my sunshine away." I think of it as Mavis's death song, given the way it repeatedly delivered her to a deep, inner place of remembering and love and loss. Her relationship with that song gave it power.

Death songs have been sung throughout the history of humankind. Mohican Chief Aupumut said in 1725:

> When it comes time to die, be not like those whose hearts are filled with the fear of death, so when their time comes, they weep and pray for a little more time to live their lives over again in a different way. Sing your Death Song, and die like a hero going home. (Finney, 2011)

The American Indians sang death songs to quiet the fear that rises up when the body loses its life force. But also as a prayer for their souls. The Iroquois word for medicine is õn-nô-kwat, translated as the soul's longing for well-being. At the time of death, whether on a battlefield, from illness or old-age, the death songs acted like medicine, asserting the soul's longing for well-being, and therefore injecting power into the possibility of transcendence and survival. This was a kind of spiritual magic that has taken on different musical forms and expressions in all times.

Each of the following Native American death songs was witnessed, passed down and remembered. Imagine the Indian whose life force is ebbing away singing:

> *"Nothing lives long / Only the earth and the mountains"*
> *White Antelope, Cheyenne, Sand Creek Massacre, 1864*
>
> (Cankú Lúta, The Echoes of Sandcreek, 2009)

> *"At the time of death / When I found there was to be death /*
> *I was very much surprised / All was failing / My home,*
> *I was sad to leave it /*
> *I have been looking far / Sending my spirit north, south, east and west /*

Trying to escape death / But could find nothing / No way of escape"
Luiseno Death Song

(DuBois and Kreber, 1908)

"Lo, the Fox, the Fox am I! / Still the Fox a moment yet /
Then the Fox shall be no more."
"Tokalaka miye ca / Nakenula waon welo."
Runs Beside, Dakota, warrior of the Fox Society

(Natalie Curtis, 1987)

These songs were created by their singers in the moment, at a time when fear and loss of control threatened to take away spiritual focus. Singing these last thoughts must have brought some relief and courage. Such is the power of music carried on the human voice. The sound of one's own voice can give us assurance and company at the most perilous times.

Poems are would-be songs, and these more recently written death poems declare the Indian's very human longings and understanding as death nears:

"A little while and I will be gone from among you
Whither I cannot tell
From nowhere we came / Into nowhere we go
What is life?
It is the flash of a firefly in the night
It is the breath of a buffalo in the winter time
It is as the little shadow that runs across
the grass and loses itself in the sunset."
Crowfoot of the Blackfeet

(Hawkins-Boyle, 2012)

"Now I go, do not weep, woman
Woman, do not weep
Though I go from you to die
We shall both lie down
At the foot of the hill, and sleep
Now I go, do not weep, woman
Earth is our mother and our tent the sky
Though I go from you to die
We shall both lie down
At the foot of the hill, and sleep."

(Alice Corbin Henderson, 1991)

My patient, Mavis had no knowledge of Indian death practices, but as I presume is true for all of us, her soul longed for well-being, and she instinctively related to her song in an almost magical way that helped ease her transition.

Music helps us to be in the moment. Music helps us to truly feel what we are feeling. So often those feelings are submerged and choked off by the need to appear alright. The hundreds of dying people whom I have accompanied had the opportunity to pass through cycles of emotion and understanding, all of which needed to be experienced more fully. When fear is the prevailing emotion, sometimes the door to a rich and meaningful death experience remains closed. But if a person can pass through the fear, with love and support, the channels are then open to receiving a fuller spiritual benefit…well-being for the soul. When the body stops wanting to eat, all we can feed then is the soul. Music can feed the hungry Soul.

As Indians in the Americas sang in the throes of death, the great Buddhist yogi Milarepa of Tibet sang his spiritual teachings to his devoted disciples as he lived, and finally during his own dying. Like the Iroquois, he too longed for the well-being of his Soul, as well as for the Souls of all sentient beings. A spiritual life engenders the lifelong, gradual creation of a final death song. It is a work in progress that takes place subliminally, unseen and unheard until the dying one dares to open her mouth and sing out the final declaration. Milarepa lived a long life, spanning from 1040 to 1123. All his works, prayers, yearnings, learnings, experiences, relationships, realizations and challenges contributed to the final melodic poem that his Soul found waiting for him at the end of the long road of his life. The same can be true for any of us. Perhaps easier for an enlightened one like Milarepa, having shed all self-conscious defenses against revealing and sharing the song of his Soul, we more ordinary souls nevertheless can still learn to access our inner songs.

True to the focus of his life as a spiritual teacher, Milarepa's death song was a final lesson to the group of monks sitting vigil at his bedside. The words of this song spoke of the secret path, offering the shortest way to enlightenment. He stressed the importance of experiencing emptiness and allowing compassion to rise up within. He sang that compassion will erase the duality that separates oneself and others, leading to the realization that all beings are One. And it is this experience of Oneness that is the ultimate aim of all beings.

I find it interesting that Milarepa's death song concerned itself with the welfare of his followers, and not with the well-being of his own Soul. Having attained enlightenment during his long life of spiritual practice, it's quite possible and probable that Milarepa felt no fear, no distress, no concern for himself. He was safe in the light that radiated within and without him. His death song was his final teaching on earth, rather than a prayer for his own soul.

Miraculously, after his cremation, it is written that Milarepa reappeared briefly in an astral body radiating in light, in order to *sing one more time* for his beloved disciple Retchung, who had arrived too late for his Master's passing. Like the Christ resurrection, Milarepa reassured his followers of the continuation of the Soul's life, and from this "Mystery Body" he sang a recapitulation of the final lesson.

This song was brief, and directed specifically to Retchung, a favored student. Again, the ideas of unification and Oneness were stressed. But this time, having already passed from the confines of the physical body, Milarepa revealed that earthly life, the transitional life of soul passage through various realms of experience, and finally the next life are all of one piece. "Three united in One. Unify them!" was his last instruction, and final will.

At this song's conclusion, the yogi's body dissolved into nothingness, leaving his disciples with the miraculous experience of witnessing the continuation of the soul beyond physical death.

Unfortunately, a most important ingredient of the death song cannot be shared here: the melodic sound manifest by the vibration of the singer's own voice, upon which the meaningful words are carried into the air and throughout the entirety of the universe. We can only imagine what Milarepa's death song truly sounded like. I share his belief that the energy of those vibrations, emanating from his throat nearly a thousand years ago, continues to circulate throughout the world. If we open our inner ears, we may be able to hear the power of his song. It's interesting that the gorgeous mandalas depicting this Tibetan saint show him in a lotus position, with his hand cupping one of his ears, as if listening for the true sound. He continues to teach us to listen and to prepare for the making of our own death songs.

I imagine at this point some of my readers will be wondering how such esoteric experiences could possibly have any relevance to twenty-first century life and death. After all, we are not yogis living in caves. However, *The Tibetan Book of the Dead* (Evans-Wentz, 1960) teaches us that preparation for death and the following spiritual transition through various stages or bardos of reality is a sure way of allaying fear and transcending a needless struggle, no matter what century we live in. Fear and struggle at death are not exclusive to the ancient world. They are very much alive in today's culture of medicalized death and dying. In my hospice work, I have found that those who open themselves to an honest preparation for death can experience an easier, more meaningful end of life. The form of this preparation must take on the personal style, culture and belief system of the dying person. But the intent and substance are the same as what is offered in *The Tibetan Book of the Dead*: to open oneself to the experience at hand, to look closely at all the feelings and sensations that arise, to review all the pitfalls and revelations of one's life, and to finally trust and let go to some great power that is the seed of our true nature.

The actual title of *The Tibetan Book of the Dead* is *Bardo Thodol*, translated as *Liberation by Hearing on the After-Death Plane*. I am not a yogini. Although I am spiritually oriented, I am very much a modern woman, curious about many expressions of spiritual belief. Some years ago, I had what I call a pre-death experience while falling asleep one night. My eye had caught the twinkling of a raindrop nestled in the window screen, and as I lazily focused on that light, I felt my consciousness shift into another, unfamiliar realm, and I heard in the distance a quiet, steady humming sound. It caught my attention, and as I focused on the sound, it grew louder and louder. The amplification of the sound was unceasing, and I was gripped by its intensity, fearful that I would be swallowed up by its immense power. Just as I expected to disappear, I was thrown back into my body, very shaken and covered with sweat. Since that night, I have called that event "The Awesome Sound," for lack of a better description. Some time later, while reading the *Bardo Thodol*, it was the following excerpt that described so perfectly what I had undergone:

> O nobly born, when thy body and mind are separating, thou must experience a glimpse of the Pure Truth, subtle, sparkling, bright, dazzling, glorious and radiantly awesome... That is the radiance of thine own true nature. Recognize it. From the midst of that radiance, the natural sound of Reality, reverberating like a thousand thunders simultaneously sounding, will come. That is the natural sound of thine own real self. Be not daunted thereby, nor terrified, nor awed. (Evans-Wentz, 1960, p.104)

I was obviously not yet ready to die, for I *was* daunted, terrified and awed. I believe the experience brought me right to the edge of death; my pre-death, near-death experience. It has served as an invaluable lesson for me personally, as I proceed through life and aging, and professionally, as I assist others in their own preparation for dying. The ancient Tibetan and Native American teachings are perennial, as true in wisdom and understanding today as always. We can continue to learn from them as we face death in the twenty-first century.

Cara was a 55-year-old hospice patient, dying of breast cancer. She had achieved a spiritual stature closer to that of Milarepa's than most

people I have known, or worked with. And she was using her final
months of life in a way that seemed to raise her to an even higher
level of understanding and self-realization. Cara was, indeed, an
extraordinary woman. But she was also very much a human being
who had suffered rejection, loss and misunderstanding in her personal
world. Cara was a divorced mother of a 15-year-old daughter, who
lived with her father in Philadelphia. Cara never shared many of the
details of that parting, but I know the separation from her daughter
was a very painful loss for her. Her relationship with daughter
Katrina was difficult, and all the more difficult to repair because of
the physical distance between them. Now that her mother was in
the late stages of cancer, Katrina made an effort to visit Mom more
regularly, with her boyfriend in tow to help buffer the tensions. Cara's
relationships with her father and his second wife (Cara's mother
had been dead for 15 years) were also strained, especially by Dad's
inability to talk freely about his daughter's illness and impending
death. While her blood family fell short of providing her with the
intimate kind of sustenance she now needed in her life, she turned
to her local community of like-minded friends, who turned out in
force to care for her while she was still at home and receiving regular
clinical visits from my hospice team, myself included.

Cara loved to sing. She had sung in several community choruses
in Central Vermont for many years, loving especially traditional folk
music from diverse cultures. During the last year of her life, while
she still had adequate strength for the task, she decided to travel to
Corsica with a local choral group to share music with, and learn new
music from, singers in that country. We all urged her on, knowing
that this would be her last trip to another exotic part of the world.
She wrote to us: "The owls are singing here in Corsica, where we
study in a 16th century church!" Such a fitting observation for her
to make. American Indians regard the owl as a harbinger of death.

Cara was still young and vital, so the cancer did not take
her away quickly. We had 22 months together before she finally
succumbed peacefully at Vermont's only residential hospice facility.
Being cared for at home by her friends and neighbors became too
difficult and chaotic, so she eventually decided to make the move to
this wonderful facility a few months before she died.

Because she had time to do many last things, Cara decided that she wanted to take on one final work project: to create a volunteer hospice choir that would be on call to sing for the dying and their families. With my assistance, and lots of organizational work done by a close friend who was inspired by Cara's wish and vision, Cara's Angel Band came into being. For awhile, on good days, Cara was able to sing with them at local nursing homes, her rich alto voice adding a dusky color to the harmonies. But eventually, the Angel Band came to sing for her, as she preferred to simply listen and rest. She was a keen and insightful teacher, and from her sensitive state, advised: "Please, just simple, quiet music...learn the songs well, so each is really beautiful before you offer it...and don't blow that pitch-pipe so loudly!"

In the end, Cara had managed to share close time with Katrina, while at the same time accepting that she could not control what happens in her daughter's future life. She stopped protecting her father's difficult feelings around death, and simply died lovingly in his presence. She overcame her fear of taking strong medicines for pain and nausea. She used every opportunity to reach out and love others, as she practiced receiving loving care in return, something that did not always come easily to her. She learned how to breathe more deeply, after admitting to me that her breath often got stuck in her chest. She went through many emotional stages of dying, from clinging to the belief that she could indeed get better, to admitting that she was failing, and then on to knowing and declaring that her death was near, and that she was ready to go. Through it all, Cara continued to sing and listen to music, to share with us what it was like to die, and to rely on her deep spiritual belief to help carry her over and through. I would be hard put to cite one death song as Cara's. In a way, she *was* her own death song. One friend wrote as she was actively dying: "It's Cara's eyes that I carry with me...eyes that are filled with knowing, with glee, with huge compassion and understanding, with past sadness, but most of all with love. She has this way of loving you with her eyes."

A favorite song of Cara's, an old American Shape Note tune (Schindler, 1841), sung many times by Cara's Angel Band (which still brings music to bedsides, six years after her death), makes this plea:

"Let music charm me last on earth
and greet me first in heaven."

So perfect a sentiment for this wise woman, who managed to bring peace to us all when she declared in her own words: "It just gets holier, and holier!"

As I researched historical contexts for the death song, I was surprised to find it appearing within Western Christian culture in eighth-century England. Bede's death song, although probably not actually sung at the monk's death, was penned by one of his students during the final hours of Bede's life. There is a lilting rhythm within the lines that lends itself well to melody, indeed:

"Before the dread journey which needs must be taken
No man is more mindful than meet is and right
To ponder, ere hence he departs, what his spirit
Shall, after the death-day, receive as its portion
Of good or of evil, by mandate of doom."

(Cook, 1902)

Much later, in eighteenth-century Boston, the Reverend George Whitefield wrote his own "Funeral Hymn" as he was in the final years of his life. In this case, he assigned the words to a hymn tune composed by Methodist preacher Charles Wesley. Whitefield's funeral hymn was sung at his funeral in 1770, as was his wish. Here it is, in part:

"Ah! Lovely appearance of Death!
No sight upon Earth is so fair
Not all the gay pageants on Earth
Can with a dead Body compare.
With solemn delight I survey

The corpse when the spirit is fled
In love with the beautiful clay
And longing to lie in its stead.
How blest is our brother, bereft
Of all that could burden his mind!
How easy the soul that has left
This wearisome body behind!…
This heart is no longer the seat
Of trouble and torturing pain
It ceases to flutter and beat
It never shall flatter again…
What now with my tears I bedew
O! Might I this moment
My flesh be consigned to the tomb."

(Wesley, 1807)

The culture, the language, the style are clearly different from the death songs of Native Americans and the great Tibetan Buddhist. However, the sensibility is the same: the soul's longing for well-being, the hope for relief from life's suffering. These prayers at life's end are common to us all, regardless of time in history or cultural background.

I met Martha in a nursing home where she spent her final years, about a year before she died. She was 89 years old, a gracious Southern lady and widow who had been long married to a Protestant minister. Martha was an educated woman, and although suffering from a degree of dementia, still retained a curiosity about poetry and learning and music. Before our relationship began, she had spent too many hours in front of the television set, almost constantly blaring in the common parlor, with little else to do.

It seemed to have demoralized her and made her more anxious than need be. She was gradually declining from gastric cancer, losing more and more footing with each passing week. But, when stimulated and supported, her mind awoke to the shared poetry and songs we explored together. I was amazed at just how many old song lyrics she was able to recall, with little faltering. She also recited poetry, remembering the old pleasures of reading (her poor eyesight made reading no longer possible), imagining the scenes each verse described. Sometimes her memory did fail her, and she would become frustrated, saying, "Oh, I used to remember so much more!" One day, as she rested, I recited poems by Elizabeth Barrett Browning, a recording of Japanese flute music playing quietly in the background. The spoken poetic word coupled with lovely music can create a vivid, theatrical experience. Martha was moved to tears and transported to some other less painful place while she listened.

One day Martha confessed that she had always wanted to take voice lessons when she was younger. But with the demands of a family to raise and a busy husband to support, she never had the time. I assured her that it was never too late for some voice lessons, and proceeded to teach her the basics of deep breathing, what every singer needs to know. Even though Martha's lungs were old, her enthusiasm about learning something new at this late stage helped her to focus on the task, and her results were pretty satisfying. She remarked with her eyes a-twinkle: "Well, dreams don't just crash and burn after all!" We worked on a few of her favorite songs: "I Dream of Jeannie" by Stephen Foster, some old Christian hymns, and finally "The Lost Chord" by Arthur Sullivan. While she was still able, we tape recorded "The Lost Chord" in her room. "Isn't this fun?" she exclaimed, "I can do it some, can't I? I want my daughter Penny to come to my next lesson." Martha's family was so grateful for the way the musical experience brought their mother back to life for a short while, and for the measured doses of happiness it added to her lonely and sometimes difficult days.

Martha eventually succumbed to the late stage demands of the cancer, and to the frailty of her very old body. She slept most of the time, and at one point she hadn't woken or spoken to anyone for several days. We all thought she was nearing death, but as I sat and sang at her bedside, her eyes fluttered and she briefly joined me in singing "Dites-Moi," a lovely little French love song we had often sung together. She remembered every word, then fell back into a deep sleep. The attending staff were amazed, as was I. At her deathbed, her family and I sang Martha's old songs in harmony, and I offered "The Lost Chord," perhaps the closest thing to Martha's own death song:

> *"Seated one day at the organ*
> *I was weary and ill at ease*
> *And my fingers wandered idly over the noisy keys;*
> *I know not what I was playing*
> *Or what I was dreaming then,*
> *But I struck one chord of music like the sound of a great Amen.*
>
> *It flooded the crimson twilight*
> *Like the close of an angel's psalm*
> *And it lay on my fever'd spirit*
> *With a touch of infinite calm;*
> *It quieted pain and sorrow,*
> *Like love overcoming strife,*
> *It seem'd the harmonious echo*
> *From our discordant life...*
>
> *It may be that Death's bright angel*
> *Will speak in that chord again;*
> *It may be that only in heav'n*
> *I shall hear that grand Amen.*
> *It may be that Death's bright angel*
> *Will speak in that chord again;*
> *It may be that only in heav'n*
> *I shall hear that grand Amen."*

(Proctor and Sullivan, 1858)

The hearing sense remains intact through the last moments of life, unless it was damaged or lost during previous years. At the deathbed, I've always assumed that I can be heard, even though the dying person appears to be asleep or in a pre-death coma. So when a person nearing death can no longer sing her own song, I can sing for her. In Martha's case, I had come to know her well, so the song choice was obvious and fitting. In other cases, I may have been called in at the last minute, not knowing much at all about a person's life. But often family members were present, and could fill me in on what was most important to their loved one. Choosing a death song for another feels like a large responsibility, but I have come to believe that the power of any number of gentle songs, those that get to the heart of what we all seem to long for at life's end, the soul's well-being, will always be right. Knowing a little personal history, orienting myself to the particular spiritual belief (or not) of the dying, trusting in my intuition and intent to provide assurance and calm, all these ingredients help me create a musical bridge for the one who is crossing, and sound-solace for those who are in attendance and grieving. This is powerful, privileged work I do. It makes a difference.

Two

The Relationship

"If only we could just simply admit that we all suffer sometimes,
and that we're really here to take care of each other."

*Closing words of a eulogy I gave for my Uncle Jay
who took his own life in loneliness and isolation*

Several years into my hospice work, I took on the supervision of a
graduate student in music therapy who wished to learn something
about working with the dying. Like many people, she had little
personal experience around death, and was eager to learn. She spent
an academic year with me, traveling around the county, observing
my work with patients, eventually contributing musically and
therapeutically to the sessions. I recall our first patient visit together.
It was in a nursing home where I often visited folks, individually
or in groups, and on this day I was meeting a new patient for the
first time in her room. Willa, my student, was tense and excited,
and I could see that she needed some assurance before we entered
the room. So we did some deep, relaxing breathing together out in
the hallway, and I reminded her that all she needed to do for the
next few weeks was to be respectfully present, and to observe. A
brief look of relief crossed her face, and I said, "OK, let's go meet
this lady."

One day, not too long into our supervision, Willa said to me:
"How do you do it? How do you just walk in, so calm and assured,
unafraid?" It was an important question, one I've thought a lot about

since. The search for the answer led me to a clearer understanding of my concept of the therapeutic relationship. Willa reminded me of *my* first meetings with new patients early in my career, and the nervousness *I* sometimes felt when knocking on a door. Indeed, it took time and many experiences to truly learn how "to be" with these folks, in the deepest and calmest sense of that infinitive. In our work together, I hoped to teach Willa that all the particular skills of music therapy: instrumental and vocal competence, developed musical expression, comprehensive repertoire, counseling and listening skills, therapeutic assessment and setting goals were hers to learn and master, from her various teachers at the university. Perhaps she would learn something about these things from observing my work. But I emphasized that it's the *relationship* between caregiver/ therapist and a person who is dying that is at the heart of it all. And learning how to be in-caring-relationship with a patient (and often family) is perhaps the most demanding and important part of being able to do this work well. His Holiness the Dalai Lama has said: "The more you are motivated by Love, the more Fearless and Free your actions will be" (2012). Learning how "to be" with patients, with people, with yourself, takes many years, lots of risk and practice. Most important is that generic kind of Human Love of which His Holiness speaks, which can lead to freedom and fearlessness. A friend and colleague of mine calls it "inner disarmament," a phrase that well describes the visceral feeling of openness and calm that I try to cultivate in my life and my work. Being with people in this state enables them to relax and open more as well, something that is necessary if any healing is to occur.

I expect that when a dying person agrees to see a music therapist, on the recommendation of his doctor or nurse, he may not know what to expect. Or he may have expectations of something very different from what I have in mind. Many people think that it's my job to entertain them with music, and although we may cross into that territory of enjoyment together from time to time, I always hope to bring something much more than that to our encounters. In our first meetings, I explain that I use music as a medicine, as a way to help them through whatever it is they may be experiencing as they face the end of life. The main reason why I can now enter a patient's home or room for the first time without fear is that I've learned to have no particular expectation about how he will respond to this offer. What I do expect is that the patient will determine just how honestly or willingly he takes advantage of this invitation to look at, and share, what he is going through. I know that it will take time to develop trust between us, so I let him set the tempo, taking cues from what he says, what his body movements tell me, what I intuit and sense as we get to know each other. I am not afraid to use the words death, loss, disease, pain...but he may be uneasy with that, and I must sometimes tread very carefully. Occasionally a patient is *so* ready to hear those words coming from someone's lips (especially if a doctor or family is uneasy about speaking openly), he is surprised and thankful for the opportunity to show himself honestly. My job is to be flexible and open, to follow my patient's lead, while staying strong and calm as he faces what is perhaps the biggest challenge of his life: to prepare for death, while living out his final days. My hope for him always is that he will be able to find meaning, satisfaction, deep connection with loved ones and inner peace during this end-time, whether it be days, weeks or months. But the only thing I can reasonably expect, at the beginning of each of these relationships, is that this person will find a way to die that he himself is capable of, and that I will accompany him as best I can.

In the 1970s, while I was teaching piano and accompanying soloists, I came across an important book entitled *The Art of Accompanying and Coaching* (1965) by the late great Austrian pianist and conductor, Kurt Adler. It was the first book of its kind published since the early eighteenth century, most probably because musical accompanying, though not an obscure role, is one that tends to be less noticed or acclaimed. The deep insights he shared guided me well during that phase of my work, but they continued to be relevant even as my musical work became more therapeutic. In my introduction I wrote about the relationship between accompanist and soloist as a metaphor for the relationship between music therapist and patient. In each case, it is the accompanist or therapist who is responsible for setting the tone for the kind of teamwork that will follow. The results of this intimate association will depend largely on the attitudes that the accompanist/therapist brings to the experience. Adler writes so wisely about this approach:

> The specific art of accompanying and coaching lies in the ability to deeply feel the soloist's intentions and his artistry; to attune oneself to his artistic style; to recognize his artistic shortcomings and to make up for them by extending a helping hand to lead him, giving him a sense of artistic mastery and matching it by following him. In short, the art of accompanying and coaching is a continuous give and take… A real artist must be humble. Vanity has been the core of many virtuoso careers but it has also been the end of genuine artistic growth… All these things would not be sufficient (without) a good deal of sensitivity… The understanding of what makes a particular artist tick may be valuable to the process through which the accompanist must go if she wants to become one with the artist. But rarely can an artist be read like an open book. (Adler, 1965, p.182)

When I work with a dying person, it is *his* intention or purpose that is paramount. I must attune myself to *his* style of communicating and *his* way of activating his intention. I must be aware of his weaknesses in achieving his purpose, and support and guide him with my skills and strengths. I must allow myself to be led, while recognizing the times when a more assertive shift of direction on my part may better serve the ultimate goals of understanding, meaning and comfort for my patient. I must not dominate, but guide. I must strive to be humble while witnessing what is often a powerful and mysterious transition in a person's life. I must remember to ask for whatever spiritual guidance is available to me before every encounter, since I know I couldn't possibly do this work well by myself. And finally, I must rely on keen senses and intuition to give me clues about what is needed, what this person is truly feeling, and what I need to do or not do in response. How interesting that I could just as easily write these words in describing the purely musical experience of accompanying a singer at the piano while performing Schubert's *Lieder*.

Music is a language. When deep conversation and sharing is impossible, because of fear, reluctance, difficulty finding the right words, music can help bring to the fore whatever is being concealed or held on to by one who is suffering. I have often broken a ponderous silence by simply singing "Nobody Knows the Trouble I've Seen," the old Black spiritual. No introduction or explanation is ever needed. My listener is often able to hear my message of compassion, to recognize that I know he is hurting inside, but unable to declare it. That beautiful, plaintive song often breaks through a defensive barrier and gently invites the tears to flow. Words are not always needed, and in this moment a deeper connection is made between us. Interspersing our encounters with the language of music diminishes stress, when using words to reveal oneself feels too dangerous. Wordless emotion is given an opportunity to be felt. We can marvel at and share the beauty and sadness together in a way that talking does not quite reach.

Recently I was playing gentle classical piano music in a chemotherapy clinic waiting room. There were a half dozen people waiting for their names to be called, some reading magazines, some staring at the wall in front of them, alone in their own thoughts and feelings. A young woman moved from her seat to be a little closer to the piano. As I played Bach and Debussy, she sat on the edge of her seat, head down, obviously listening. In between pieces, we said nothing to each other, but I felt her attention and presence clearly and deeply. After about 20 minutes, her name was called, and she looked up at me before leaving, tears streaming down her cheeks. She said: "That was beautiful. Thank you." I can only imagine what her story was, what she has lost, what she may fear, what she may hope for. But I did not need to know the details. The language of music made it possible for her to feel deeply what she was experiencing, and we connected, however briefly, in a meaningful and intimate way.

Listening is such a big part of the therapeutic relationship, practiced not only by myself, but by the patient. The little story I just told is a good example of how simple listening can unlock emotions that need to be expressed. But it's also a good example of how *my listening* to *her listening* enables me to establish a very close connection with her through the music. My awareness of, and attention to, her response to the music helped support her through the experience, without any words, or any movement on my part from the keyboard. We communicated on a level that is psychic and extraordinary, one of the mysterious ways that music can bring us in close relationship. This is, indeed, potent medicine.

Nel Noddings, the educational philosopher, writes that a caring encounter has three elements:

1. A cares for B—that is, A's consciousness is characterized by attention and motivational displacement.

2. A performs some act in accordance with #1.

3. B recognizes that A cares for B.

(Noddings, 2002, p.19)

Both teaching and practicing therapy have some common goals, perhaps most importantly the improvement and welfare of the student or patient. Building upon a foundation of true caring, which requires an act of full attention and openness, is necessary for real success. Without that, trust will never be established. When I began playing piano in the clinic waiting room, I was focusing on my music, yes, but my primary focus was on the needs of those patients in the room with me. I watched while I played, and waited for any signs of responsiveness.

It's interesting that Noddings uses the word "performs" in the second element of caring. For her purposes of describing the execution of an act that indicates a desire for connection and relatedness with her student, it suffices. But in describing the act that I offer in a music therapy situation, the word "perform" is loaded with all kinds of connotations that I believe are inappropriate, and not at all helpful. Performance by an artist, a dancer, actor or musician implies a presentation of high achievement, the enactment of some feat that is somewhat extraordinary, a "show" of talent. In modern Western culture, we revere performers as stars, heroes, and shower them with accolades and praise, especially when they are highly accomplished. Although performers engage in their art for the love of it, there are ego benefits that accrue as a result of success, for better or worse. In the realm of therapy, this kind of relationship between listener and performer is not what I have in mind when I offer patients my music. My "motivational displacement" is to offer the listener a *gift* of something expressive and beautiful. Yes, it is something that I create as an accomplished artist, but the focus is not on how wonderful a musician I may be, nor on any wish for accolades or applause. This is the act that I offer to establish connection with another, the basis of which is my caring for their welfare. That is very different from ego-driven performance.

This is not an easy concept to teach people. Some of my medical colleagues still use the word "perform" when talking about my work. And those patients who expect entertainment may think of what I am doing in those terms as well. It takes time to teach this new way of thinking about and experiencing the sharing of music. And that, too, is part of my job. In ancient Egypt, women priestess-musicians called shemayet (musician) or heset (singer) offered music in the sacred temples. Because the early Egyptians did not separate their spiritual belief from their practice of medicine, vocal incantation played an important part in the healing process. The shemayet were revered, not as stars, but as keepers of powerful mysteries and healers of the highest order. Their offering of music was inextricably bound with both medicine and the sacred.

When I played Bach for the woman in the waiting room who was clearly engaged, it was in that shemayet-spirit that I offered the music. As a result, she felt no need to get up and pat me on the back, to clap her hands in appreciation. She simply lifted her head and showed me her tears. In that moment, our eyes met and held each other, and I knew that my intention to convey caring had been successful. She recognized it, was moved to express feeling, and was deeply thankful.

One of my musical heroes is the late Juliette Levin, who was one of the early pioneers of modern music therapy in Europe. She was a very accomplished classical cellist who brought her considerable musical talents to the service of all sorts of people who suffered mentally and physically. She also created a very important school of music therapy in England in the 1950s, when this field was just getting off the ground. I mention Levin because she could have easily had a successful concertizing career, so beautiful and accomplished was her playing. But she instead devoted her work to helping others, while using "performance" skills in conjunction with a deep sense of caring and a sharp aptitude for therapeutic intervention.

I admire her work because the quality of the music she gifted people with was of a high caliber, artistically. One of the concerns I have about young music therapists who are sent out into the world today is that they sometimes fall far short of this level of musicianship and artistry. I believe that people who are suffering deserve the most beautiful music we can make. I truly don't disparage anyone who plays several guitar chords and sings in a simple voice. Lots of good work is being done with simple musical means. But my hope is that more music conservatories will offer training in therapy so that the most accomplished musicians will follow a path of offering music in service to others. The world of high performance in concert halls is suited for some, but it is also a rather exclusive family of artists. I continue to work on my own musicianship and classical piano skill, so my gift will be the most beautiful it can be. I think that high quality and beauty get people's attention. St. Thomas Aquinas wrote, "Beauty arrests motion." Something lovely can stop patients in their tracks and hold their attention. From there, we can begin to build trust and get on with the work at hand.

While we therapists can aspire to musical perfection (never possible!), we should also learn to expect occasional musical mistakes. Learning how to notice them as they happen and breeze along with the music without self-consciousness or self-blame, is an important skill in developing a solid relationship with a patient, as well as ease in playing. Responding with acceptance and humor when we mis-step is one of the hardest things for any of us to learn in life. It is humbling, in a good way, and reminds us that we are simply humans, learning and growing all the time, right until the moment we die. For one who is at life's end, it's helpful to be reminded that we can only do the best we can do, and that is never perfect. Behaving with that reality in mind is truly heroic, I think. Living and dying in that way is noble and manageable at the same time.

Jean was a middle-aged piano student of mine when we first met. She had studied piano as a child and adolescent, then given it up, as many young people do, to follow other interests. In Jean's case, she eventually became an accomplished equestrian. She enjoyed classical music and vintage songs, such as Hoagy Carmichael's "Stardust," and hoped to reclaim some of her rusty and nearly-forgotten piano skills. Before I practiced music therapy in medicine, I taught piano privately for many years, focusing not only on musicianship, but also personal and emotional growth for the student. I often found myself working with adults, such as Jean, who had had somewhat negative and unsatisfying experiences with childhood piano teachers, and hoped to bring music back into their later lives in a more joyful way. So, in a sense, my teaching involved a certain kind of therapy that used the musical experience as a vehicle for self-growth.

Life is full of surprises. It was through my relationship with Jean that I was introduced to the world of end of life care. Neither of us knew it at the time of our meeting, but Jean was soon to be diagnosed with glioblastoma, a fast-growing brain cancer that so often leads to death within a relatively short period of time. This was terrible and startling news for this otherwise very healthy woman, who decided that she still wanted to carry on with piano lessons as planned. As the universe would have it, I had recently completed a training in volunteer hospice work, learning the basics of end of life care. But I hadn't followed up with doing any actual volunteering with the local hospice. Perhaps I was subconsciously waiting for Jean to show up.

Several weeks into piano lessons, both Jean and I noticed that her left hand was weakening. The tumor was located on the right side of her brain, and this was only the beginning of the gradual loss of much of her left-sided mobility. The specific location of the mass eventually affected both motor and cognitive strength, and within a few months it became clear that Jean needed daily care and support. Lessons in my studio could no longer continue, but Jean had begun to trust me as a teacher and friend. And my interest and caring for her as both a student and a woman of my age who was dealing with a very serious life-threatening disease led me to take on the role of part-time "companion," which Jean and her husband offered as a paid position in their home. Jean and I agreed that we'd keep music alive in this new arrangement, which we could easily do, given the baby grand piano in her den. Her husband, already quietly grieving and at a loss as to what to do to help her, immediately went to work building a sunroom addition onto their old country house, a place that included a fine sound system where Jean could listen to music and rest, and, sadly, eventually die.

I had ten months to learn, from Jean, how to build a caring relationship with one who is dying. It was one of the longer therapeutic relationships I've experienced with a person, and perhaps the most intense because I spent five mornings every week with her. I got to know her as a very private, lonely individual, who had spent much of her lifetime trying to fulfill the expectations of others. She seemed to have no close friendships. During those ten months, I recall only one friend coming to visit her, and only once. Several family members paid visits, especially during her final weeks, but Jean did not seem to share very intimate connections with any of them. Indeed, even her husband spent most of his time working outdoors, constantly mowing fields and lawns, repairing equipment, clearly avoiding close contact with the daily losses his wife was facing with me inside the house. No blame. He channeled all his fear and grief into working outdoors, the best way he knew how to cope with such a devastating change in his life. Occasionally, Jean and I would venture out for a little walk, waving to Jim in the field as he drove the tractor, before her initial minor stumbling led to the need for a cane, and then a wheelchair.

I accompanied Jean through two brain surgeries, followed by two cycles of chemotherapy, all the while watching her clutching onto shreds of hope and not able to yet give up on what even her doctors knew was a futile attempt to save her life. After chemo treatments, we'd return home and Jean would immediately go to the couch in the den. I would play gentle piano music while she slept. Several days of deep fatigue, nausea and vomiting would follow. We used music to calm and soothe her. She would sometimes cry as I played. But for the most part, she was reluctant to speak in words what her deepest fears were. I let her take her time with this, until one morning when I saw that her panic and desperation could be contained no more.

Jean had just seen the results of the latest MRI showing no reduction in the size of the tumor. In fact, even with chemotherapy and all the distress she had undergone to get through it, the mass had continued to grow. I was with her when her kind doctor shared these results, and gently let her know that he was running out of ways to help her. Even then, Jean believed that she was "expected" to continue therapy, expected by her family to fight for her life. I doubt that this expectation was ever clearly verbalized by those who cared about her, since this family was not very openly communicative. These may have been expectations that Jean had created in her own mind, based on past experiences and what she may have believed the world at large expected of her. Or perhaps some in her family did have these attitudes, spoken or not. In that moment of panic and desperation, Jean cried out: "I don't think I can keep doing this!" I took her hands and said, "You don't have to keep doing this. You can stop fighting. You can decide to stop chemotherapy, to find some peace before you die." She looked at me incredulously, as if the idea were totally new to her (as I'm certain it was). She answered: "I can stop?" I took her hands, smiled, and said: "It's all up to you, no one else."

The relationship we had forged made it possible for us finally to speak honestly about what *she* needed to do. I helped her get hospice services in place, she said farewell to the oncologists who had tried to save her life, and Jean spent the next few months at home, enjoying small pleasures, listening to beautiful music and saying goodbye to those she loved. I sang and breathed with her at her bedside as she drifted into a deep coma and died on her own terms.

My relationship with Jean was long, multi-faceted, and very intense. But some of the relationships with hospice patients that followed, after obtaining my position on the clinical hospice team, were very brief, some as brief as 45 minutes. Bearing in mind the simple practice of calm focus on the patient, as well as the situation at hand, I learned that I could address the most important thing that was needed, even in the last hour of life.

One afternoon I was called to the deathbed vigil of Winifred, an elderly resident in a nursing home. She was attended by her two sisters, both elder women themselves. I had never met Winifred before, and I quickly assessed that she was nearing death. Her eyes were closed, she was not verbally responsive, and her breathing was shallow, rapid and touched with audible congestion. Her two sisters looked sad and worried, noting that Winny hadn't said anything to them for the past two days. They needed to know that she was OK, but their sister hadn't given them any sign that she knew they were there with her. I assured them that Winny did not appear to be in distress, that her manner of breathing was a symptom of her body shutting down. But they remained anxious, as I began working with Winny, sitting at her bedside and close to her ear.

I always assume that the one dying can still hear me. Hearing is the final sense to go, so I can use the ability to communicate with a patient through this channel until the very last breath is taken. So I spoke very gently and clearly to Winny, told her that I would be breathing with her, in her own body's rhythm, for awhile, and hoped that this would be OK with her. No overt response, but I began anyway. Each time Winny inhaled, I inhaled with her. And each time she exhaled, I exhaled with her. After several rounds, I added a simple audible tone on each of our exhalations, so that Winny could actually hear me breathing with her. Gradually, her breaths deepened a little and slowed down in tempo, and my breaths followed suit. This is a good sign that breathing in tandem has helped a person relax a bit. Knowing that someone is "laboring" with you must be a great relief at this stage of the dying process, when a patient can no longer speak and may feel isolated, even though others are present.

The two sisters watched anxiously as I continued this simple breathing and toning with Winny for several more minutes. Suddenly, I heard a faint tone coming from her throat as we exhaled together. She repeated it at the next exhalation, and the next, until

I was certain that she was indeed toning with me. I encouraged her to let out that soothing sound each time we exhaled, that she was doing just fine, and that the vibration she was emitting would help to soothe her as she went through this transition. Her sisters, by this time, had scurried closer to the bed, holding each other and, like birds, chirping little sounds of amazement and joy. "She hears us!" one exclaimed. "She knows we are here. And she seems to be alright." I assured them that she was, and that now would be a good time for them to sit with her and tell her what they wanted her to know. After saying my grateful goodbye to dear Winifred, I left the three sisters to their final communion. Winny died peacefully 45 minutes after I left.

It is not the quantity of time spent in a caring relationship that is most important. It is the quality of attention and response to exactly what is needed at the time that leads to truly helping people. The outcome of my long relationship with Jean was no more successful or meaningful than the outcome of my very brief relationship with Winifred. Music and sound played important roles in each case, coupled with a way of being with people that allows the real issues and needs to emerge in their own way, in their own time. This open, attentive, calm way of being in a challenging situation allows trust to develop, either gradually or almost instantly. Trust makes it possible for us to approach death in relationship, facing it more honestly and calmly. Like a soloist and accompanist, we can make a kind of music together, until the last notes are sounded and the one who is dying takes her final bow.

Three

Some Things the Dying Need to Do

"Work for the night is coming
Under the sunset skies;
While the bright tints are glowing,
Work for daylight flies.
Work till the last beam fadeth,
Fadeth to shine no more;
Work while the night is dark'ning
When man's work is o'er."

American Civil War hymn, 1864, Anna Coghill and Lowell Mason

Most hospice patients have foreknowledge of their deaths. I say "most" because now and then someone is admitted to hospice care in the very last days or hours of life, when conscious awareness is waning. But for those who know that death will most likely come within weeks or months, the period of time ahead can be a fruitful one. Knowing that death is just around the next turn often leads to anguish, anxiety, fear, withdrawal. But it can just as often lead to an urgent desire to make use of the time left in meaningful ways. When I was a little girl, one of my favorite songs was "I'm Gonna Live, Live, Live Until I Die," sung by Frankie Lane. Whenever I visited my French grandmother, Même Beatrice, I'd sneak into the parlor that was closed off for special visitors and place the 78 rpm record on her old Victrola. Frankie's soaring voice made me dance and dance like a whirling dervish. Even at age six, the words of the song had special meaning for me. So now, when I encounter a patient who uses her foreknowledge as an opportunity to "get to work," I think I know what that's all about.

Reviewing one's life seems to be a task that many folks need to take on. Whether it occurs within their own private thoughts or more overtly with the help of an interested listener, looking again at one's personal stories, especially the ones that brought joy, sadness, a feeling of accomplishment or the shame of failure, a memory of great pain or loss, or the experiences that taught us important life lessons, seems to be a way of reaching a sense of completion, acceptance and understanding at life's end. This seems especially true for those who have lived long lives, and have many memories to sort through. For those who die younger, at mid-life, and who mourn the loss of more years ahead, more experiences to accrue, it may still be an important way to lend value to the limited time they had. I wonder if very young children also have this need to review, assess and complete, even in a simple way. I have known of hospice children who spent their last days comforting and consoling those around them, like little wise caretakers of the bereft. It strikes me that in their innocence, it may not be quite so necessary to reconcile the events of their own little lives.

We have all heard stories of near-death experiences, where a person comes back to us describing the light-speed review of her lifetime as it flashed before her mind's eye the moment before the car hit the tree, or just before her heart stopped on the operating table. When there is no foreknowledge of death, the life review seems to take place in the blink of an eye. But for many hospice patients, this process is lengthened and carried out in weeks or months. Whether super-fast or leisurely, this activity seems to be a necessary, almost instinctive urge before we die. Whether it is programmed within the brain, the mind or the soul to do so, I cannot say. But it seems to be a powerful way to reach peace and self-understanding at life's end.

My friendship with hospice patient Gus had a long opportunity to deepen over the nearly two years that I knew and worked with him and his wife, Hilary. Six months is considered a long hospice stay, but Gus continued to live on, long beyond the time his doctors had predicted. So, although he didn't often feel very well, he had plenty of time to finish his unfinished work. And he was quite clear about what he needed to do.

Gus was 82 years old when we met, living through a slow decline from prostate cancer which had metastasized to his bones and kidneys. His more serious physical complaints were shortness of breath, having to be on oxygen much of the time, and generalized bone pain, which was managed somewhat by regular chemotherapy. Gus often said that he never wanted to take chemotherapy, but he was "a sissy for pain." Over time the side effects of this treatment, fatigue and mental fuzziness, were unacceptable to him, so he stopped chemo and became a full-fledged hospice patient. Though he continued to decline over the months that followed, in many ways his life improved, in that he was better able to focus on the final projects that were important to him, activities that gave him a good measure of satisfaction and fulfillment in his last days.

Gus was a tough man with a soft heart. We had several important traits in common, and hit it off together right from the start. His ancestors were Scots people from Canada (mine were French Canadians), he was a descendent of the Sauk Indian Black Hawk (my blood relatives were Mohican and Mohawk). His sun sign was Scorpio, as is mine, which lends itself to deep passions, strong character, a love of being alone. He had been born and raised in his grandparents' farmhouse in the Mad River Valley, and would end up dying there. Gus was a true folklorist, storyteller and song maker. He had kept a written record over his long life of many personal adventures, was in the process of finishing a family memoir with the help of a niece, and had a collection of simple original songs recounting his days as a semi-professional boxer, an aviator in World War II, a farmer and logger and mason. He had transcribed many old songs he had heard his mother sing when he was a youth, hoping to keep them alive after he died. The remarkable thing was that all this work was kept in cardboard boxes in his little office. It had never been shared with *anyone*. At long last, Gus wanted to share all this treasure with me. So we got to work.

The second time I visited, Gus was all set up in the parlor with a small table before him, his box of writings on it, and a rocking chair for me. As he showed me his song lyrics, he confessed that he was shy to sing in front of anyone. But with a little coaxing and a big show of interest and curiosity on my part, he sang through one of his favorites, "The Hobo," and then waited expectantly for my response. What a wonderful vignette about his days in the ring, when he was known in the boxing circuit as The Hobo. What a wonderful, deep baritone voice he had! And how hard he worked to summon the breath he needed to sing! I was ecstatic, and I let him know. A big beaming smile spread across his face. We were on our way.

We decided to tape record as many of Gus's original songs as we could, and from that day on, he joined me in singing his song-stories while I added autoharp, tambourine or medicine drum accompaniment. Each song brought with it reminiscences of days gone by, and Gus always filled in the gaps with verbal storytelling. He had known Jim Jeffries, the famous American boxer of the early 1900s, had fought in boxing matches in Los Angeles where W.C. Fields was the emcee. He eventually went to war, learned to fly airplanes, and kept that love alive for many years in a small private plane he owned. At age 30, he married very young Hilary (16) and raised a family of four children on the old farmstead. When he wasn't farming or logging or building masonry structures, he operated a one-chair lift at the Mad River Glen ski slope. Gus knew everyone in the Valley, and he was a beloved neighbor and friend to many. This vast array of experiences had been chronicled by Gus over the years. Now was the time to share, to reveal.

As the months passed and the assault of illness besieged him more and more, Gus shared that he was "fed up," was "ready to die," but hoped "to die in my sleep." He worried about the physical and emotional toll this was taking on Hilary, who had her own health issues to deal with. The trust between us finally made it easy for him to shed tears. It seemed that one of the very few positive things left in his life was our work session, now attended by Hilary who sat off in the corner of the parlor, quietly crocheting her beautiful afghans. Despite his growing weakness and continuing pain, Gus always rose to the occasion, sang his songs into the microphone, and found an hour of enjoyment and great respite from his troubles. Singing delivered more oxygen to his tired lungs, elevated his mood, supported the review of his fascinating life, and lured his shy wife into the world of his creative self.

Finally, the day arrived when Gus stopped singing and took to his bed. I sat by his side as he was dying, and sang lullabies and sweet songs of peace. At his funeral, inside a packed church in the village, Gus's rich, deep voice was heard over the speakers singing a tender love song he had written to his wife many years before; a fruit of all the recording work we had done. There will always be a special place in my heart for this dear man, who modeled so well the need to live purposefully until death. One of the last things Gus said to me was, "The Hobo wishes you good luck."

The Hobo

Step right up and take your bow
You're meeting with the Hobo now
Win, lose or draw, you soon will know
You've met a fighter: The Hobo

You may be the best of friends
But in the ring the friendship ends
For in the ring, you will recall
The Hobo has no friends at all

There was a girl the Hobo loved
He quit the ring, hung up his gloves
And then they moved where few would know
He was the fighter, The Hobo

Some final projects are much smaller, but no less important to the person who needs to get it done. Ethan lived deep in the wild hill country of Vermont on the way into the Northeast Kingdom. A more authentic mountain man does not exist. He lived alone with his dog in a house not far from his adult children on a muddy back road that wound through the forest. This was a hard-working, hard-drinking clan of loggers, devoted to each other in their rough way, and Granddad Ethan was watched over faithfully by his sons and daughters and grandkids.

Ethan was 89 years and 4 months old, as accurately reported by him on the day I asked. He usually said that he felt "worse than some, better off than some." His long, scraggly beard nearly covered the bib of his old overalls, and one side of his face was shrouded by a large brown malignancy. Although he suffered from COPD, a serious pulmonary disease, he continued to smoke his hand-rolled tobacco, while he rocked in his chair by the big pot-belly woodstove. He was a fiercely independent guy who had lived a rugged life, and wasn't about to do anything he didn't want to do, especially at this late stage. Ethan's hospice nurse sent me to meet him because he had told her about a song he had written to the tune of "Big Rock Candy Mountain." He called it "Woodbury Mountain," the place where he lived, and he wanted to make it a Christmas present for all the young'uns before he died. So out came the tape recorder again, and even though Ethan was nearly stone-deaf, he still could sing his song. It went like this:

> *I live on Woodbury Mountain*
> *in a wooden shack*
> *with an ugly dog*
> *and a wild cat*
>
> *Way up on Woodbury Mountain*
> *where the birds and the bees*
> *and the chigger red trees*

and the lemonade springs
where the bluebird sings
Way up on Woodbury Mountain

Way up on Woodbury Mountain
you'll never change your socks
where little streams of alcohol
come trickling down the rocks
and the lake of home-brew has whiskey too
you can paddle all around in a big canoe
Way up on Woodbury Mountain

Way up on Woodbury Mountain
the cocks have wooden legs
and the bulldogs all have rubber teeth
and the hens lay hard-boiled eggs
where every day is Sunday
and the squaws do all the work
so all we have to do
is carouse around and shirk

Ethan lived to pass on his little recording to his family at Christmas. And then a few weeks later requested another ten copies to give to his neighbors. What a hoot he was!

Once life has been subject to the dictates of medical treatment, some folks simply long to return to normalcy. Being able to again do some simple activity that was part of easier and happier times can be a great blessing for those who are dying. Such was the case for Rosamonde, an 89-year-old French Canadian lady who lived alone in a modest house in Barre, Vermont. She was enduring the final few months of gastric cancer, a terrible illness with particularly difficult symptoms that test anyone's craving for dignity and comfort. The morning I crossed the threshold of Rosamonde's home, I felt like I'd returned to my own family's ethnic history. Like many elders in the Granite City, she had emigrated here from the neighboring province of Quebec as a child, bringing with her and retaining throughout her life the many provincial customs of her native land. She spoke English as haltingly as I speak French, and when I greeted her with "Bonjour, Madame!", and she followed with an endless, very rapid response which left me in the dust, I had to immediately warn her that "Je parle le Français, mais très lentement" (I speak French, but very slowly). We both laughed and shyly carried on. Like my own French relatives, Rosamonde was a bit suspicious and reticent around people who are not from their small community. But when I revealed that my own Même and Pêpe were from French Canada, she dropped much of her guard and complimented me on my good French grammar.

I always love having to tap rarely used language skills. French speech is so musical and lilting. Like my hometown of Fitchburg, Massachusetts, where many French people emigrated to work the paper mills in the nineteenth century, Barre, Vermont is home to the French and Italians who flocked here in the same century to work the granite quarries. The Franco-American community there still hosts a wonderful music and dance festival every summer, featuring the responsorial songs and foot-stomping dances so popular with the country folk in French Canada. Taking Rosamonde on as my patient gave me another chance to taste and play the music of my own heritage at a time when she needed to be lovingly reminded of who *she* was and where *she* came from.

During our first visit, after assessing some of Rosamonde's needs, I finished the session with a couple of French songs. She was delighted, exclaiming "J'aime la musique." This lady was clearly depressed, lonely and worried about what was ahead. Seeing her smile in response to my singing gave me the clue I needed to take this a step further. I asked if I might bring my portable piano for our next visit, so I might sing more French songs for her. She immediately asked, "Puis-je inviter mes amis pour le concert?" (May I invite my friends for the concert?). "Bien sûr!" (Of course!),

I replied. Rosamonde reminded me just how important at-home social occasions are for the French. They needn't be fancy, but they are always opportunities for the hostess to take care of her guests, indeed a customary way to express love and friendship. In her final weeks, Rosamonde wished to do one more time what she had probably done many, many times in her life. And this time, she would have live entertainment!

Knowing that her days were numbered, we scheduled the event for the following week. Rosamonde greeted me at the door, dressed in her best "Sunday clothes," despite her extreme thinness. She had wisely invited only four guests, who were already seated on the sofa in her parlor, munching on chocolates from the candy dish. I set up the piano, all the while attempting to converse with this highly loquacious group of Frenchfolk, surrendering when their speed got the best of me, and wondering what they were saying *about* me when I just couldn't keep up. I apologized for my slowness, and they in turn replied (as had Rosamonde the first time we met), "You have good French grammar!" I'm sure I did not fully appreciate the nuance of that remark. I suspect it was their way of saying, "You speak French (Parisian dialect) differently than we do (Québécois)." Nevertheless, we enjoyed laughing together. We were ready to begin "the concert."

I sang and played, to their delight, for close to an hour. Songs such as "La Vie en Rose," "La Violette," "Hymne à l'Amour," "J'étais Petite Mère," "O Canada, Terre de nos Aïeux," "Le Ruban de la Mariée," and "Ave Maria" (en Français) filled the little room with the sounds of homeland, calling back memories and making space for many emotions. For that hour, Rosamonde was able to put aside her worries, share moments of joyful recognition with her friends, and leave them with a parting gift. I know she must have taken to her bed early that evening, tired from all the excitement. The little party continued even as I rolled the piano out the door. It was the last time I saw Rosamonde. Although I called and spoke with her daughter about visiting one more time before her death, this wonderful lady who reminded me so much of "my own" was too uncomfortable and withdrawn to see me again. I think we left it as it should have been: a sweet memory, for all of us, of a lovely musical soiree.

Eighty-nine-year old Opal had much the same idea when she asked, "Is it OK if we invite some of my friends to come and listen to the music? No reason to waste it just on me!" Opal was a fiercely independent country woman who didn't let severe glaucoma and congestive heart failure slow her down much. A very different personality from Rosamonde, she was matter of fact, down to earth, no-nonsense, and self-deprecating. She had worked in the Cabot Creamery in younger days, raised a family, and now lived alone in a small elder housing facility on the outskirts of Cabot Village. She and seven other women each had their own small apartment, were fast friends, and supported each other in many ways, as good neighbors do in rural Vermont. We all met in the common room, Pearl provided simple refreshments, and these hardy women sang along to old familiar songs, accompanied by me on piano and Willa (graduate intern) on guitar. Shakers and drums filled in the beat, and we created our own homespun "kitchen tunket." We all had such a good time, we repeated this group session on several occasions before Opal's illness finally slowed her down. Good medicine for one turned into good medicine for many, thanks to Opal's generous nature.

The death of an elder is often sad, but not necessarily tragic. A long life reaches its end, loved ones mourn, and the generations left behind continue on. But too often in hospice care, folks in mid-life and younger fall prey to serious disease, and a life is cut short before more has been realized and experienced. We all wish for many years, even though life can be hard. But when that is not in the cards, we call it a tragedy. Such was the case for Tina and Joe, a married couple in their mid-fifties. Both had been previously married, Joe twice, to women who had both died of cancer. He had been through a lot of emotional loss in recent years, and when he learned that his high school sweetheart was divorced, the two reunited and married. Tina and Joe were in love, and had found new happiness together. But it only lasted for a few months after their marriage, when Tina learned that she had ALS, amyotrophic lateral sclerosis, sometimes known as Lou Gehrig's disease. ALS is a progressive degeneration of muscular strength that travels throughout the body, often leading to death within a few years. Some people live with this incurable disease for a longer period of time. But Tina was not one of those people. She died a mere ten months after being admitted to hospice and palliative care.

Tina loved music, had recently taken a classical music appreciation course, and enjoyed the piano music and song I brought into her home. She was already in a wheelchair, gradually losing her ability to speak and swallow. Joe watched over her day and night, quietly mourning within as he witnessed the love of his life approach the end of her days with him. The energy of love and loss was palpable in their household. Shakespeare himself could not have conjured a sadder love story.

One day, after playing music for Tina alone, I wondered if there might be some way to include Joe in a musical experience that fit the two of them. I suggested to Tina that we might create a romantic interlude some evening, where the two of them could sit close together on the love seat while I played love songs from their youth on the piano. Tina was excited about the idea and said she would invite Joe on this "date." Although a shy and quiet man, Joe accepted the invitation and we made plans for the special evening. Candles were lit, wine was poured, I set up the piano a respectful distance away from the couple across the large livingroom, and Tina and Joe snuggled and listened to "Love Me Tender," " Goodnight Sweetheart," " Norwegian Wood," "Scarborough Fair," and other gentle songs of love and longing. An hour of sweet sounds cannot turn tragedy into a happy ending. But I think it helped them to find comfort in one another, as each bore their own private grief about hopes unrealized.

It's difficult to understand why a person like Joe was besieged with so much repeated loss. After Tina died, my hospice team worried a lot about him. He had hidden himself away in their country home, and began to drink heavily. Our attempts to support him through his accumulation of grief were rejected by him, and he simply asked to be left alone. Within 18 months, Joe was admitted to hospice care, dying in a nursing home of a cirrhotic liver. When I was called in by his nurse during the last few days of his life, Joe was withdrawn, depressed, bitter and close to death. I asked if he'd like me to sing at his bedside, and he refused. "I just want to go." Soon after, he lost consciousness. I held his hand and breathed in rhythm with his body, toning audibly on the outbreath so he would know someone was there with him. The pain of living can break people. Joe made his choice, and I bid him a fond farewell, without judgment, indeed with compassion and sadness.

One of the most courageous things one can do before dying is to admit failings, and to ask for forgiveness. I haven't seen it happen often, but when it does, it can make an enormous difference in just how much more peacefully one can let go of life and say goodbye. It also allows those left behind a feeling of completeness, relief, making more space for loving memories. We can repair damaged relationships even on the brink of our dying, just simply by acknowledging a wrong committed in the past, and by saying "I am so sorry. Will you forgive me?" But this takes great courage on the part of the patient, and strong support from one, like myself, who is an objective but caring partner in the process.

Stewart was in his late seventies, lived alone in a small hilltop home with a magnificent view of distant mountains. His hospital bed was set up in front of a large window that took it all in, filling the place with light and pastoral loveliness. His adult daughter Laurie, in her forties at the time, had left her own family behind in Portland, Maine to come and care for her father. She had a strong Christian belief, and even though her childhood history with Stewart was a painful one, she nevertheless felt that she needed to honor and care for him in his final few months, suspending her own personal life in order to do so.

Stewart and Laurie enjoyed listening to piano music and songs, especially old favorites from the American musicals. One day I sang "You'll Never Walk Alone" from *Carousel*, which especially touched Stewart as he gazed out at the mountains. It became a theme song of sorts, which I repeated each time we met. Eventually, Laurie started to share with me privately some of her childhood experience with her father, which involved his leaving the family when she was quite young. Their relationship had been stiff and stressed since then, and because Dad had never acknowledged the suffering he had caused her and others, she continued to feel deep pain. She admitted to me that she truly longed to be able to forgive him for leaving her so long ago, especially now that he was dying of cancer, but she just didn't know how to do it. He had never said he was sorry, and without that, she couldn't take it further. I so related to this sad woman, who had needlessly suffered many years because of her father's probable guilt, shame and inability to admit to hurting those he loved. My relationship with my own father was very similar. Little did I know, I would be facing the same challenge in a few short years while caring for *my* dad as *he* lay dying of cancer. I assured Laurie that I would do what I could to facilitate a meeting of hearts and minds between her and Stewart in the coming weeks.

One day, not long after, at the conclusion of "You'll Never Walk Alone," I knelt down on the floor next to Stewart's wheelchair, and talked to him about his daughter. Laurie was within earshot, working at the kitchen counter. I said to Stewart, "You know, your daughter has taken such good care of you, has been so generous to give you her time. You must be grateful and proud." He admitted that, yes, he was. I continued, "Laurie has spoken with me about some needs *she* has, and asked if I might help you two talk about it." Stewart was receptive, and I invited Laurie to join us in conversation. I had to say very little to help get things going between them, simply that there were old hurts that needed mending. With this, Laurie was able to explain to her dad just how painful his leaving had been when she was a girl. She wanted to be able to let go of that pain, and to forgive him, but wondered if he was sorry. Stewart's eyes brimmed with tears, he reached out for his daughter and took her hand. His apology was immediate and heartfelt, in fact Stewart appeared so relieved at being given the opportunity to reach out in this way to Laurie. She, in turn, was able to say those most important words, "I forgive you, Dad. And I love you." Stewart died a few weeks later, narrowly missing a death that could have been packed with difficult feelings of shame and regret for important things left undone and unsaid.

I cannot conclude this chapter on some things the dying need to do without telling the story of the man who simply wanted to do nothing. Carroll was a very learned and rather eccentric fellow in his forties who had contracted brain cancer. He was a high school English teacher before illness brought his career to an end, and was from an intellectual family of writers and composers. He and his second wife, Marie, had a young three-year-old daughter, Ariadne. As the effects of a fast-growing brain cancer ravished his mind and body, Carroll was thrown into a world where he no longer could command cognitive or muscular control over what he wished to say or do. When friends came to visit, it became more and more frustrating for him to attempt to meet with them in the mindful and verbal ways that once had been so important to him. A man who had once been so eloquent slowly became unable to utter the simplest sentence. His anger and frustration often exploded in the presence of his young daughter, who didn't understand the terrible fix her father was in. His poor wife became depressed and resentful, exhausted from changing the diapers of both a toddler and her husband, who was returning to an infantile state as quickly as Ariadne was growing away from it. This family needed some relief.

Next to Carroll's narrow bed in the family room was an old upright piano with a few broken keys and not in the best of tune. Knowing about Carroll's love of all things artistic, and especially classical music, I kept my talk with him to a bare minimum. The only things I wanted to ask of this poor man were that he lie back, close his eyes and listen. Perhaps expecting that I, another hospice worker, might be there to demand something much more complex from him: answering questions about his symptoms, inserting a catheter, practicing physical therapy exercises, Carroll looked truly surprised and asked, "That's it?" I answered, "That's it. I'd like you to do almost nothing at all, Carroll." He smiled, lay back, and listened to a lovely, symmetrical, flawlessly complete Scarlatti sonata for the next several minutes, perfectly quiet and serene. When it was done, he opened his eyes and said, "*I can do nothing. So easy!*"

As I followed Carroll from his home into a nursing home, I continued to play whatever piano was available. He, and sometimes his brothers, listened quietly to Mozart and Debussy and Bach and Scarlatti, without the need to utter a word. Like a Buddhist monk, Carroll gradually slipped into his world of nothingness receiving the great relief and sustenance that beautiful music has to offer. I hope he came to realize that doing *nothing* can be as rich and full as doing *everything*.

Four

The Safety of Culture

"Home, home, sweet sweet home,
There's no place like home, There's no place like home."
Henry Bishop and John Payne, from the 1823 opera Clari, Maid of Milan

Throughout our lives, we continually long for the feeling of safety. Living is difficult, every day is filled with challenges. We often find ourselves having to deal with something new and unfamiliar, which may lead to a sensation of being adrift, unsure of how to chart a course that will bring us back to a safe harbor. Each day after our labors we return to home, whatever and wherever that is, to reclaim that feeling of the familiar, of safety. We hope to achieve calm and rest so we can meet the challenges of the next day. This is the safest place we know, a nest that recreates for us, at least subconsciously, the ultimate feeling of safety within the womb, that sublime state we enjoyed before we were born into the world.

As one approaches death, this longing for safety may be most keenly felt. Having worked with a vast variety of people at end of life, I have noticed that even the most devoutly religious folks experience a degree of apprehension and uncertainty about what lies ahead. After all, even allowing for the possibility of reincarnation, either we have never died before or we cannot recall the experience of having died before. It feels as if we are approaching the unknown, the most unfamiliar thing we can imagine.

We are about to fall off a high cliff, which doesn't feel very safe at all. We hope and pray that we will fly when we reach the cliff's edge, but who knows? Until that time comes, we continue to yearn for the feeling of safety, as we make our transit through physical and mental decline.

Spending one's last days and months at home is a good way to begin cultivating a feeling of safety. Another powerful addition to end of life care that has the same effect is highlighting and practicing the customs and culture of the patient and family. Culture is just another expression of the idea of "home," the safe and familiar place. Culture contains all the old traditions, rituals, attitudes, artful expressions and social customs that, through repetition, embody what is most familiar, what is safe in each person's life. In the midst of our own culture, we know what to expect, we know how to behave, we can be at ease, we can feel connected to others in a special way. Bringing culture to the bedsides of the dying reinforces the feelings of belonging, of resting safely within the nest.

Fortunately, all cultures find expression in sound and music. Exploring the music of different peoples, different religions and spiritual beliefs, different nationalities and languages has been a fascinating part of my work. As a voice major in college, I studied numerous languages, so I already had some advantage in learning cultural songs that might reach a particular patient in a special way. As with the French woman, Rosamonde, it is always a joy to see the look of surprise and connection on the face of a patient whose original language is coming out of my mouth, in the form of a song. The language of home, whether spoken or sung, fills the air with sounds that soothe, that help us feel safe.

Vermont has been called the "whitest" state in the union. I suppose that is based on population, and the tiny percentage of people of color who live here. The most heavily populated county, Chittendon, is home to a growing number of refugees from Asia and Africa, and that's where the most obvious facial and skin variety is seen on the streets. But elsewhere, despite all the white faces, multiculturalism also abounds.

I was called to the home of Geoffrey about 48 hours before he died. There was little time to collect detailed information about this man and his family, only a warning from the nurse that he was afflicted with a massive cancerous growth on his face, and that his wife, Kristina and adult son, Jake were exhausted and in need of support. I grew to take emergent cases such as this in stride, remembering to use my eyes and ears acutely after entering the home in order to pick up cues about the culture and values of those within. I had no idea what I might offer these people, but trusted that this would become clear soon enough.

When I drove up to the house, I saw an immense log structure sitting on a knoll in the woods. It looked like a lodge, but without any particular adornment or character other than its solid, rustic architecture. So when I walked through the front door, I was amazed by the old wall tapestries, unusual furniture and ancient artifacts that punctuated the cavernous interior space. This was obviously an educated family that had traveled. The rooms were rather dark, and the home felt more like a small medieval castle than a house. I expected to see monks walking quietly about, but instead I was greeted by Geoffrey's elderly wife, who appeared to be very tired and fragile. She led me into an adjoining den where her husband lay asleep on a small bed, covered with a sheet. Although I urged her to let him sleep, she abruptly woke him, probably not clearly registering just how close to death this man was. He briefly opened his eyes and almost immediately retreated back into sleep. I urged Kristina to perhaps lie down and rest herself while I sat with her husband. She settled down in the adjacent great room, and I got to work.

Geoffrey's face was indeed a necrotic mask. I could only imagine the gentle and arduous wound care that his family, nurse and aides had to provide every day to get him through this ordeal. Sleep must have been a blessing for him at this point, and it was clear by his external signs of weakness and inability to respond that his death was near. It seemed that the support of deep relaxation through the use of very simple sounds would be helpful. So I placed a CD of hemi-sync music and sound on my portable player to set a serene mood. Hemi-sync is an audio technology developed by the Monroe Institute in Virginia which adds engineered sound waves to very lovely instrumental music in order to induce certain brain responses. I often use recordings that effectively lead the listener into an alpha state of profound relaxation, and this is what Geoff listened to as he slept.

As the music played I began to breathe with him, toning on the outbreath. After awhile I improvised my own gentle melody with the harmonies of the CD, without words, simply using "mmm" or "aaah," much like a mother lullabying a baby. As Geoff and I were floating together within this soundscape, son Jake quietly joined us to observe and listen. His entrance called me back to our surroundings, and I noticed that pinned to the patient's sheet was a very old scapular. A scapular is a monastic cloak-like garment worn over the shoulders, indicating affiliation with a religious order. A simple version of the scapular is used by the Catholic church when young people receive the sacrament of confirmation. I remember being cloaked with mine when I was 13 or 14 years old in a very solemn ceremony. The one pinned to Geoff's sheet was of this type, but it was obviously much older. I grasped the cloth in my hand as I sang, and noted a Latin prayer inscribed on the small rectangular badge. Instinctively, I added these Latin words to my melody, over and over again, until an ancient chant enveloped this bedside vigil. Nothing could have been more appropriate for this man and unusual family. No wonder I sensed the spiritual presence of monks when I entered their home.

I left Geoffrey sleeping and snoring very peacefully. His son, quite moved by the spontaneous ceremony, told me that he too was an accomplished singer, and that later he would sing for his father at his deathbed. I left knowing that I most likely would not be visiting Geoffrey again, but that his son would be able to offer him gentle songs as he slipped away.

The medieval theme took form again two days later, after Geoff had died in the middle of the night, when several family members wrapped him in a cloth, placed him on a litter, and carried him in a simple procession around the grounds of his home. This was a meaningful ritual which they had planned to do before sending Geoff's body away for cremation. It is homemade cultural ceremonies such as these that help survivors feel comfort, connection and completeness at such a sad time.

Passion is not a word usually associated with hospice patients. Passion takes great energy, it can be exhausting. The dying are more likely learning how to ration what little energy they have left; a heavy expenditure of passion is a luxury of the past. Nevertheless, passion is what I found when I met Paolo.

Paolo was 88 years "young," the son of old-world Italian immigrants who had come to America for work in the granite quarries of Barre in the early 1900s. Like his father before him, Paolo worked the quarries for many years; dangerous, backbreaking labor that too often leads to the onset of emphysema in later life. Poor Paolo was tethered to an oxygen tank, struggling for a good breath after any amount of physical exertion. But even with this limitation, Paolo exuded friendly excitement whenever his hospice caregivers paid a visit. He lived in his daughter's home, and although she and her adult daughter were fully Americanized, Paolo himself remained Italiano through and through. He spoke English with a strong accent, and I soon learned that he loved to sing Italian and Spanish operatic arias. He wasted no time in telling me at our first visit, "I love 'La Traviata,' 'La Bohème,' The Three Tenors, oh, Luciano Pavarotti! I am in heaven!" All the while gesticulating with his arms, and working himself up to a near-frenzy. A better candidate for music therapy at life's end I could not have imagined! When Paolo discovered that I could sing right along with him, in his native languages (he was fluent in Spanish, as well as Italian), he was delighted, and more than ready to get to work.

Our plan was simple: Paolo would undergo a nebulizer treatment with his granddaughter's help 30 minutes before our sessions each week to clear his lungs and ready himself for singing. I would bring musical scores of his favorite songs and arias, and we would work on them together. Now, I knew of course that Paolo's condition would not allow him to sing in full voice. Robust and clear singing requires strong lungs and the ability to breathe deeply and to control exhalation. Yogic breathing is quite similar to this process. Sadly, the ravages of emphysema would not permit Paolo to learn this kind of breathing technique. But that was not my aim. I saw how his mood was lifted, and sometimes soared, as we sang "La Paloma," "Core 'Ngrato," "Torna a Surriento," and "O Sole Mio." He was especially happy to have the musical scores in his hand, which motivated him to read and speak and review the Italian and Spanish lyrics during the week in between sessions. He called me his "music teacher," and said, "You are the best thing my hospice nurse has sent me!"

Paolo's family was so pleased to see their patriarch enjoying happy times in his final months. Eventually home care became too difficult, and Paolo went to a nursing home to give his family some much-needed respite. I followed him there, and we would work at the piano together, Paolo still attempting to sing a little from his wheelchair. After awhile, he simply listened as I played and sang to him and other patients who would often gather round. Paolo would always proudly say to them: "This is my music teacher!"

The day Paolo died, I sent a small group from the hospice choir to sing for him in his room. He was confused, a bit agitated, but still wanted to comment on the singing, and tell everyone how he had been working on his songs. The light of passion for his cultural and musical heritage continued to shine, albeit dimly, even on his last day. Buona notte, Paolo. Could it be true that perhaps you heard the sweet strains of an Italian aria as you left us?

Culture is not determined only by language, skin color, religious practice, customs. Cultures are created by groups of people who also share common behaviors, attitudes and traditions. Within the population of Vermont, there is a large subculture of hunters and woodsmen. Our state is full of natural beauty, abundant in wildlife, veined with clear waterways and rivers and blanketed by hard and softwood forests. Many people who live here prefer being outdoors to indoors. Johnny and Peg were a part of this culture.

Johnny was a 65-year-old guy hit with early onset dementia. He and Peg had married a bit later in life, were very much in love, and had shared many outdoor adventures together. They lived in a camp-like house which Peg had transformed into a comfortable home, along a back gravel road in a small, hardscrabble town. Johnny had been a master hunter, trapper and angler, and Peg, herself a tough woman who loved the woods, accompanied him on many hunting trips near and far. When I first met this couple, I found Johnny lying in a hospital bed in the main living area, surrounded by mounted trophies on the wood-paneled walls. Johnny wasn't an ordinary deer hunter. He had tracked and taken down great moose and bear, large bucks and wildcats. He used the pelts and otherwise ate what he killed. Like many hunters in Vermont, this man kept alive an ages-old tradition of hunting and trapping, and had become a master at it. Although not part of this culture myself, I had to honor and admire the accomplishments of this man and his wife, who appreciated the natural world in a gritty way and who displayed their pride in this endeavor on the walls of their home.

Johnny had trouble speaking intelligibly and was now favoring staying in bed most of the time, given his weakness. But every now and then, he would make a very clear declaration, usually one sentence. Peg would hold on to these expressions and share them with me whenever I visited, so we could both understand better what Johnny might be going through in *his* ironic state of entrapment. One day he said: "I'm standing in line, standing in line to go home!" Another time, while I was with him, he blurted out a pretty raunchy expletive. Peg scolded him, but I cheered him on. He had plenty to be angry about.

Johnny enjoyed having me sit at his bedside while I sang songs about nature, old traditional tunes about the wilderness, songs about country fairs and courting. Even while sleeping, his finger would tap in rhythm with the music. Peg would lie next to Johnny in his bed and stroke his head. She said: "This music session and visits with my therapist (one of my colleagues) are the best things for me. It's so good for me to just stop taking care of everything, to lie down and snuggle with him while we listen together." Peg had the good sense to hire another younger woman to help with Johnny's care, and as caregiver Janet became closer to this couple, she too was invited by Peg to lie next to Johnny on the other side of the bed. He obviously loved it, and it did us all good to see him smile. This was such loving generosity on Peg's part, and in many ways throughout their ordeal, she was a model of the best kind of caregiving.

I eventually learned that Johnny had been a Catholic altar boy in his youth. So one day I played my shruti box, a small droning bellows instrument that is used for chanting. It has a very haunting and soothing sound, which accompanies nicely vocal improvisation. As the shruti box droned in a perfect fifth, I sang a melodic version of a portion of the Mass while Johnny listened and rested. I thought the Latin words might help awaken in him a memory from his past. So I sang a responsorial prayer, shared by priest and altar boy:

> *"Emitte lucem tuam et veritatem tuam:*
> *ipsa me deduxerunt et adduxerunt in montem sanctum tuum,*
> *et in tabernacula tua."*

> *"Et introibo ad altare Dei:*
> *ad Deum qui laetificat juventutem meam."*

> *"Send forth Thy light and Thy truth:*
> *for they have led me and brought me to Thy holy hill*
> *and Thy dwelling place."*

> *"And I will go to the altar of God,*
> *to God, the joy of my youth."*

(The Ordinary of the Catholic Mass)

Johnny simply rested and slept as I sang that day. But at the next visit, Peg excitedly told me that several times since then Johnny had begun to sing in a "strange way." She thought that the words might have been Latin.

In this case, I became as close to Peg as I did to Johnny. She confided in me that she was a recovering alcoholic, and that she was so thankful to be able to now feel her feelings, given the emotional intensity of this episode in her life. The music I brought reminded her to practice all the good stuff she had learned through Alcoholics Anonymous. Bedside music always brought her to tears, sometimes made her laugh and smile, always intensified the love she felt for this man to whom she was so beautifully devoted.

So, at Thanksgiving time, when Johnny and Peg would ordinarily have been in the woods tracking deer for the winter freezer, Johnny breathed his last peaceful breath while Peg lay by his side. This Latin-chanting, foul-mouthed hunter found his peace in the loving arms of a remarkable woman.

Cultures are not always old and long-practiced. Some, like the so-called counterculture of the 1960s, are newer creations, often borrowing from ancient traditions, but also building something fresh for a "New Age." I'm never certain what to call the cultural group in which I myself feel most welcome and comfortable. "Counterculture" may have been descriptive and more appropriate 50 years ago when many of us were young adults, and were indeed resisting or countering the pulls of a much more conservative American culture of the mid-twentieth century. The wonder of this new culture is that it has carried on, changed, grown and matured throughout the past decades, and it enjoys a strong presence in Vermont. We no longer counter with the rebelliousness of youth, but coexist with those of different minds, all the while strengthening our own way as we continue to educate and work with others. Many vanguards of this culture, people like me in their mid-sixties, came to this state in the 1970s to settle down and raise families. We now have adult children with young children of their own, so we are becoming three generations strong. We tend to be well-educated, active in progressive politics, spiritually oriented in a personal way, very concerned and involved in ecological sustenance and survival. We prefer organically grown foods, indeed some of us run organic farms or work in co-ops. Natural medicines and herbs often line our bathroom shelves. Some have home-schooled their kids, others are public school educators, artists, musicians, writers, shop-owners, carpenters, loggers, tradespeople. We live in cities, we live on remote mountaintops. Like Johnny and Peg, we tend to love the outdoors, but instead of snow-mobiling and four-wheeling, we run, hike, cross-country ski, snow-shoe. Living simply and as naturally as possible, while honoring each other and the planet we inhabit, is a common creed. Sometimes we are referred to by others, with tolerant humor, as the "Crunchy Granolas." I think of us as a growing tribe of interesting, caring, peaceful people, who work hard to keep this ethic and culture alive.

I walked into such a home of peaceful souls a few early springtimes ago, where the matriarch grandmother, 87 years old, was dying of advanced Alzheimer's disease. Polly had three adult daughters, a son, and a flock of grand and great-grandchildren. She lived in an old, quirky farmhouse in the middle of a small village, surrounded by overgrown flower beds and vegetable gardens. Her adult children, most especially her three daughters, had been watching over their mother for weeks, working as a team, bringing their young children along to help. It was a warm, busy family scene, where Polly's peace and comfort were of paramount importance. Polly had a small room to herself, located just next to the busy kitchen where something was always cooking on the old stove or baking in the oven. Friends and neighbors would come by in groups of twos or threes and respectfully sit with this beautiful, old woman as she slept. Sometimes the young children would spend a little time with Grandma as well, coloring on the floor, quietly playing with toys, but always very calm and peaceful themselves. These children were not "sheltered" from the realities of dying, the sad prospect of losing a dear family member, nor were they deprived of the pleasure and happiness of hearing the old stories of her long life that reflected the important role she played in all of their lives. In the midst of the room, Polly lay on a small bed, her long white hair flowing over the pillow, dressed in an old-fashioned cotton nightgown and covered with a colorful, homemade quilt. I loved joining this lovely, warm scene, and the family delighted in listening to me sing and play old Shaker hymns, Buddhist and Native American chants, vintage love songs and gentle classical piano works.

Polly had been a painter, and her daughters had adorned the walls of her little room with many of her paintings, mostly scenes from her garden or other natural vistas. Polly had read the Eastern philosophers and had lived her life according to the realization of the impermanence of things earthly and the endurance of things spiritual. She mentioned the Sikh teacher Kirpal Singh in her advance directive documents, giving us all a clear direction to follow while administering her spiritual care. One of her daughters, who had sung with our hospice choir, requested a visit from the singers. So I was able to arrange for a choral visit a few days before she died. This was indeed a homemade, custom-designed death vigil, one that suited this great mother and her descendants beautifully.

Polly and her children practiced meditation, so when I used song in tandem with deep breathing and toning, Polly responded easily, reaching deep states of relaxation. One daughter told me that at times her mother would hum simple little musical phrases, repeatedly, even though she was too weak to speak or stay fully alert. Polly seemed to use her breath and voice instinctively to create a soothing vibration within her body that would help her remain comfortable. One day, she quite unexpectedly sang out: "Hey there, you with the stars in your eyes!," which prompted her daughters to find the song on the Internet. I know it from my childhood in the fifties, and her family was struck by how sad a love song it is. I sang part of the song for them. It prompted them to tell me how their alcoholic father left them in the 1950s, when they were living in California. It had been a very difficult and sad time for Polly, and this spontaneous musical expression from Mom reminded them of the sorrows they shared as a family, as well as the triumph of recovering and becoming whole again. In a lighter vein, on another day, a brief strain from "Go Tell Aunt Rhody" flowed from Polly's pale lips, foretelling that "the old grey goose (would soon be) dead." Even in her failing state, she made us all laugh at her barnyard humor through a simple phrase of a song.

As the days went by and Mother's care became more demanding, the sisters still continued to work as a team, generally refusing help from hospice aides. They knew that *their* touch would help Polly the most. The hospice nurse offered and urged them to use morphine for discomfort, as needed. But Polly had requested that this be done sparingly, so she might remain as alert as possible at the end.

Her daughters found a good compromise, using the medications to relieve any obvious suffering or breathing difficulties at the end, while relying on calm music, gentle touch, soothing words and the gentle spirit of this household to reinforce the peaceful composure that Polly appeared to be able to maintain for the most part on her own, because of her spiritual practice.

After Polly died, the family transported her body themselves to the crematorium, created their own burial ritual, and mourned and celebrated their mother in the same homespun way they all lived. Their creative loving-kindness and adherence to a chosen culture brought deep meaning and peace to all of them at the completion of Polly's life.

The writer Nancy Banks-Smith (2011) writes: "Cultural anthropology is the science which tells us that people are the same the whole world over, except when they are different." As a musician working with multi-cultures, I've become an amateur ethno-musicologist, digging into the vast musical literature of the world to find fitting sounds to administer as medicine to the dying. But even while honoring people's differences, I am constantly reminded of the common ground we stand upon. We all are born, live and die. We all group together for comfort. We all experience and, it is hoped, share joys, sorrows, disappointments, fears, satisfactions, triumphs. The flavors and textures, musical or otherwise, of these human experiences may vary in beautiful and colorful ways, but the source is the same: human beings creating together a framework in which to make sense of a world of constant change, indeed, a life of indeterminate length, in which we all wish to feel safe.

Five

Difficult Emotions

"My skin is back upon me,
and my bones are burned with heat.
My harp also is turned to mourning,
and my organ into the voice of them that weep."

Holy Bible, Book of Job, King James version, 30: 30–31

Perhaps the most emotionally charged predicament of human life is the certainty of impending death. All hospice patients, whether or not they are able to consciously and unhesitatingly admit it, know that the end of life is nearing. The emotions that rise up out of this knowledge are not easy to ignore, though some people may try to dismiss or even hide them. The constellation of emotions can be complex, confusing, even chaotic, ranging from calm serenity to intense rage or gripping terror. At a time when a failing body is losing strength, it is asked to incorporate the physical manifestations of a variety of emotions, some of which are difficult to bear. I have rarely seen a dying person totally at peace with the prospect. More often, those preparing to die are tested by the necessity to digest a thick stew of distinct, and sometimes paradoxical, emotions. Music, like the wick of an oil lamp, can draw out emotion like little else and help to bring order to inner chaos.

Cherie was in her early forties, gradually wasting away from ovarian cancer. She was a tough woman, accustomed to dealing with the hard circumstances of her life. She had been married, beaten and abused by an alcoholic husband, divorced, and then blessed with a child challenged by developmental disabilities. Her young son was taken from her by the state for reasons unknown to me. He was the one possibility in her life for something good, something positive, and she had to settle for visitation rights. Cancer at early mid-life was the last blow she had to endure. She was a very angry, tortured woman.

Cherie was taken in by her mother, who lived in a small trailer on a back road, for the final months of her life. Visiting this patient and her extended family was an eye-opener for me. It was early in my career as a hospice therapist, and although I had seen plenty of poverty and hard circumstance in my life, Cherie's lot was remarkable for its recurrence of bad times and loss. I met with her on six or seven occasions before her death, and whenever I visited, the front porch was always full of sisters, brothers, aunts and uncles, all smoking, sometimes drinking beer, lots of kids in the yard, pick-up trucks and old cars parked every which way on and off the dirt driveway. It struck me that Cherie's time of dying was not only a sad family event, but a good opportunity to gather and "party," in a strange and cynical sort of way. Perhaps it was a personal drama they didn't want to miss. Or maybe it was the only way they knew how to band together and get comfort. Rarely were her relatives, other than mother, at her side. It was summer, and Cherie stayed indoors, close to the bathroom and her hospital bed, even though the trailer remained stiflingly hot from the humid heat. This woman, her life story, her disease, the social and physical environment were terribly disturbing, and it all provoked both compassion and aversion within me for the suffering and coarseness all around.

Intense situations require intense remedies. Gentle, beautiful, calming music was not going to help here, at least not until Cherie was in her final hours. Her seething anger at the injustice of her life demanded a musical response that honored and acknowledged her right to feel difficult emotions. She also needed a way to express herself more fully, to perhaps unload her body of some of the heavy burden of unresolved rage. Our talks were mostly about her son, her marriage, and the trials of her disease. But one day she lit up a bit as she told me how she used to love to dance. Hard-driving rock 'n roll was what inspired *her* body to move. And in its own irrepressible way, I'm sure it also served to blow off a lot of pressure and steam during her hard and stressful life. So, I asked if she thought she might be up for just a little more dancing. And she agreed.

As I prepared for Cherie's "dance session," I thought of the songs of Alanis Morissette, a Canadian alternative rock singer/songwriter, who emerged into the American pop music scene in the mid-1990s. Alanis sang her outrage and angst with a compelling wail of a voice, backed up by a gritty, driving band. Her lyrics were never nice. The unfailing honesty of her expression has always been scorching, almost embarrassing. She fearlessly sings the uncensored emotions of many women. Listening to her music has always helped me to dig deeply into my own emotional pain. It seemed perfect for Cherie.

I brought two recordings of Alanis with me to our next session, along with two fluffy, goose down bed pillows. Despite Cherie's growing weakness, she was determined to hear and dance to this special music. I cleared a small area in the crowded trailer, closed the door to the porch, and started the music at a robust volume. The song was "Sympathetic Character," a seething declaration of all the things a woman is afraid of in her abusive partner: his physical dominance, the humiliation he caused her, his stink of alcohol, his total disregard of her. In the final verse, the woman rises up and claims her own rage and pain, shrieking out the agony of keeping her own emotion under wraps. The music is harsh, the story is one shared by too many women throughout our violent world, Cherie herself being one of them. I invited her to start moving her body to the rhythm, any way she was able, as I beat a tambourine at her side. Her tall, reed-like body began to sway, first in very slow motion, then with a bit more energy. She closed her eyes and let herself go, surrendering to the pulsing, passionate words of a terror-stricken woman.

I handed Cherie one of the pillows and showed her how to whack it to the floor, against the chair, against the bed. With her last reserves of strength she injected some of her rage into her flailing movements, as the song reached its breathless end.

I guided Cherie into a comfortable chair where she rested, spent and exhausted by her effort and expression. As she closed her eyes and her breathing found a new rhythm, we listened to Alanis' heartbreaking ballad, "That I Would Be Good." This song, so different in tone and energy from the first, expresses a child-like longing to be seen as good, fine, and loveable, despite misbehaving and falling far short of perfection. Morissette's raw, unashamed voice claims her right to love even though she may be lazy, overweight, overwhelmed, clingy—even insane. It has often made me cry, thinking about our human frailties and deep desire for acceptance.

Cherie and I did not need to process this experience verbally. I think talking about it would have spoiled it. But I suspect her inner meanings had to do with a simple wish to be free of all her torment, as well as her need to be loved and deemed "good" despite illness, weakness, and the unrealized dreams for her life. Her body moved in ways that could not have been expressed in mere words, so deep was her anguish and longing. The image of her bending like a willow in a stiff wind remains with me to this day.

Two weeks later, Cherie died at home shortly after I sang gentle songs at her bedside while a hospice aide tenderly bathed her skeletal body. The time for pain and anger was finally over for her.

Unlike Cherie, whose justifiable anger was never directed toward me, but rather remained seething inside, another very different patient, Agnus, displayed anger and hostility toward her caregivers at every turn. But I suspected it might be a camouflage for other difficult emotions. My hospice supervisor referred her to me, writing: "I believe A. is isolated, angry and afraid. She is in a very good nursing facility, but manages to alienate anyone who shows her positive attention. I wonder if a gentle medium like music could draw her out and help make her whole again before she dies." It felt like a tall order to me, but nothing else had yet worked with this lady, who didn't have much time left to find some peace.

I found Agnus alone in a room at the end of a long hall, the furthest from the nurses' station. I knew the staff at this facility to be competent and caring, but still wasn't surprised that this cantankerous, complaining and ornery woman had been placed as far away from the center of activity as possible. She had effectively alienated herself from nurses and aides who had done their best for her. When I arrived on the scene, even though she continued to receive good care, staff had pretty much given up on Agnus, as much in self-defense as in demoralization. This was one of those times when I felt some trepidation myself as I knocked on her door and ventured in.

A small voice summoned me into the room. I could not have been more surprised by the visage that greeted me. Agnus was a very small, 81-year-old woman, with fluffy white hair held off her face with a decorative headband. One look at her told me that she had once been a very beautiful woman. Her skin was still smooth, probably from years of good care and expensive lotions. She was alone in her single room, resting in bed, her body modestly covered by a pretty nightgown and light sheets. I could not see her feet, which were riddled with gangrene. It was to be the final infection of her life, and I assume a most appalling condition for this fastidious lady to have to endure. Despite her reputation as an aggressive bully, I saw before me a tiny, aged "princess," trapped in her lonely turret.

After my simple introduction, I jumped right in: "Agnus, I've been told that you are a very angry person." My bold nature, softened by a gentle touch, has often disarmed those who might otherwise be ready for a fight, and I saw no reason not to take this risk in this difficult case. Momentarily startled by my surprising directness, Agnus looked me in the eye and, in her sweetest voice, replied, "*I'm not angry.*" She then put on her best behavior, just to prove that I was wrong, and we had a good, long talk.

I discovered that she had no family, other than a distant niece who took care of her financial affairs and visited only once a year. She had lived at the nursing home for more than a decade. She never had visitors, was friendless, and because she had resisted making good connections with staff and other residents in the facility, was truly alone. Her loneliness embittered her, and she had grown unable to trust anyone. A photograph of her husband, in World War II regalia, hung on the wall. She was reluctant to talk about her long ago past, and I suspected (rightly) that he had died in the war. With no children, and robbed of a long, married life, Agnus must have spent most of her life in a fruitless and unhealthy type of mourning, unable to recreate emotional intimacy and sustenance. At the end of her life, she may have been most angry with *herself* for missing the boat. This sad, lonely woman simply needed my attention, love and understanding. I asked if she might like to be wheeled in her comfortable geri-chair to the grand piano in the large common room during our next visit, for a private concert of special music. She surprised me with her compliance, and we made a date.

One week later, I arrived to find Agnus all ready for her concert. The nurses and aides had been forewarned about this little adventure, and had agreed to help dress Agnus for the occasion. She was decked out in her favorite blue and green print frock, hair adorned with a matching headband, tucked into a geri-chair under a pretty lap blanket. Wedged into the chair, next to her side, was her enormous handbag, full of treasures she did not wish to leave unattended in her room. She sat proudly and silently as we wheeled her to the open common room, down the long hallway which she had so rarely traversed during her years of isolation and loneliness. Heads of residents and staff turned as our regal procession passed by, I suspect as much out of awe as surprise.

The aide wheeled Agnus to her place of honor, next to the piano bench where she could see me play. I opened the lid of the grand, invited her to simply sit back and listen and enjoy, and then began to play. The common room was very lovely, built in a rotunda style with large windows framing the pastoral scenery of green mountains and valleys. For the next hour we enjoyed the lighter piano classics of Grieg, Scarlatti, Mozart, peppered with old vintage love songs from the nineteen thirties and forties, "Stardust," "I'll Be Seeing You," "Always." Agnus especially liked the older songs from Broadway, music from the shows *South Pacific* and *The King and I*. It was a full program of delightful pieces which eventually drew the attention of other residents and staff, and halfway through the concert the big room was filled with other wheelchairs scattered about, occupied by her neighbors. The smile on Agnus's face as she held her place of honor was unforgettable. I am looking at a photograph of her on my desk as I write this, a gift of an aide who captured the image to mark this little event.

In the next few weeks that followed, my new friend and I repeated this musical ritual, even as she began to show signs of her final decline. In the meantime, Agnus's attitude toward other staff improved almost miraculously, and the nurses and aides warmed to her again. She shared with them a very old portrait of herself as a young woman with beautiful, flowing dark hair, rosy cheeks and dancing eyes. It must have been taken just before the loss of her husband, when the promise of life and happiness was still before her. The nurses hung it on her wall for all to see, and Agnus proudly shared it with me as I visited and sang at her bedside in her final days.

My hospice supervisor had been right to hope that music, special care and attention might help this lady to find peace and wholeness again before she died. Not only the patient experienced a kind of healing in this case, but a medical staff was guided toward reconciliation with someone in their care. We all won, myself included, as we worked as a team to get beyond anger, distrust and hostility. I believe Agnus died in peace.

Responding to personal attention and creative intervention, as Agnus did, enabled her to shed some of the difficult emotional defenses which were not serving her well at end of life. Like a wilted flower after watering, she attained a higher, more comfortable state of being. In a sense, she "didn't know what hit her." She did not *intend* to make a change in herself. Her soul's unconscious longing for well-being simply responded to a quality of energy provided by an exterior source, if you will. I have witnessed this kind of change many times in my work, so powerful is the effect of well-applied energy medicine. This is not hokus-pokus magic. It is the very real effect of injecting calm, compassionate, focused energy into a difficult situation.

On the other hand, I have rarely seen one who is dying *consciously* take on the hard work of changing a personality disorder that has ruled attitudes and behaviors for an entire lifetime, in the interest of growth and a better death. Most people die as they have lived, helped by the strengths they've already cultivated and hindered by their weaknesses and shortcomings. For them, it is enough to get through the disease process any way they can, for better or worse. That, in itself, is a valiant achievement. But another patient, Maddy, showed me that working toward essential psychological change in the final stage of life is indeed possible.

I met Maddy when she was 53 years old, living temporarily (she hoped) in a nursing home facility, and just beginning to digest the knowledge that metastatic breast cancer would eventually cause her death. The cancer had spread to her bones and abdominal region, leading to intermittent pain and nausea which was to increase over the coming months, necessitating careful management with opiates and other drugs. She had already been through several years of fighting cancer with chemotherapy and an array of alternative medicine therapies, but to no avail. The fighting phase was over, and she realized that preparation for dying was the next hill she had to climb. She agreed to hospice services and decided to give music therapy a try. Music was something she loved, along with painting. She expressed a hope that "it might help."

Along with her serious physical disease, Maddy packed another serious challenge. She lived with obsessive-compulsive disorder (OCD), a behavioral syndrome that attempts to cope with alternating bouts of intense anxiety and depression. It was a well-ingrained, and necessary, facet of her personality and modus operandi. Not an easy way to live, but it had gotten her through 53 years of life's challenges. Unfortunately, OCD was not going to be a great ally in getting through the challenges of dying. A healthy preparation for death, as I know it, asks that we learn how to relax, accept and finally let go; behaviors and attitudes not that easy for one *without* OCD, and perhaps next to impossible for one, like Maddy, *with* OCD.

Upon meeting, she presented a stern, critical and controlling persona. She occupied a small, single room in the facility, which was beginning to get cluttered with as many of her belongings as she could fit in, all precisely placed. Everything was in extreme order. Whenever I came for a visit, she would ask me to move the extra chair to a specific spot, and then return it to its "home" as I left. These were the early days, when we were just beginning to get to know each other. Thankfully, we ended up having 16 months of regular time together, during which some of these emotion-driven behaviors softened and changed.

Maddy was a loner, despite the fact that she had sisters, mother and a "boyfriend" nearby. She received visits from these people throughout her final months, but often complained about how disappointed she was in her family's inability to be honest about her illness and impending death. Her boyfriend was perhaps her best support, but he too suffered with debilitating depression and anxiety, most likely the common trait that brought them together. Barney was also an art lover and painter, an avocation which they could enjoy together. Many of his paintings decorated the walls of Maddy's room. Although these familiar people did their best to offer support, Maddy felt like their implied message was that *she* take care of *them*. She was always ambivalent about upcoming visits. It became clear over time that she depended on me to be her most trusted support.

Our sessions together always included listening to recorded music. Maddy was intelligent, curious and eager to learn new things. We used her own library of relaxing music frequently, but she wanted to listen to the new music I suggested as well. The peaceful sounds of nature music, hemi-sync music, spiritual and New Age music always accompanied our talks, foot massages, and drawing exercises. I was surprised and pleased to discover early on that Maddy was quite open to hearing my honest assessment of how her controlling attitudes and behaviors could get in the way of finding peace before she died. She was willing to start practicing something new, one tiny step at a time.

Over the weeks and months that followed, we tried many things. I taught Maddy deep breathing and muscle relaxation techniques. I guided her through interactive imagery exercises, where symbols of her symptoms were allowed to take form so she could "dialogue" with them about her needs. I recall one vivid session when Maddy experienced the sensations of a moist, dark, hot cave, obstructed with boulders—all images she would subsequently work with and transform to obtain more comfort. We listened to Steve Halpern's *Spectrum Suite* while feeling energy flow through our chakra centers. Maddy discovered that the process got stuck in her throat chakra, leading to the helpful insight that she had something to say that went beyond her more customary petty criticisms of others. I found a wonderful Zen art tool at a local bookstore which allowed her to sketch very intricate designs, much like Buddhist sand-paintings, and then lift a cellophane cover to make them disappear. The more beautiful the picture, the harder it was for her to let it go, but every one she drew was finally released forever. These were powerful practices that helped reinforce mentally and emotionally that it was OK and safe to relax, accept and let go. The reassuring, calming influence of music in the background seemed to support her through these unfamiliar acts of courage.

As the months went by and Maddy's condition worsened, her hope of returning home to die diminished and finally disappeared. With no reliable family caregiver to live with her through her last weeks, hospice services would be more effectively administered in the nursing home. She decided that it was time to pack up all her belongings and turn in the key to an apartment that had been home for many years. Her progress loosening the constraints of her obsessive-compulsive tendencies was not always steady and forward. For each step forward, there sometimes followed another step or two backward. But Maddy kept on fighting this dragon, leading to gains that were truly remarkable in my sight. At first, she expected to be able to go to the apartment with her sisters and pack her things the way she wanted. After two attempts to do this, she realized the task was too big for her to manage, and she turned over the physical work to her helpers, under her off-site supervision. Her orders were not always followed, and frustration and despair set in until Maddy eventually surrendered her control and agreed to let her sisters carry on in their own way. "Just please, don't lose my papers!" was her last desperate request. Letting go of home and possessions was far more difficult for her than erasing a pretty drawing on her Zen art board. The reality of losing control of her physical energy to cancer required her to give up control of the external structure and stuff of her life. It was a wrenching experience of finally letting go. But after it was done, she felt a surprising kind of relief and lightness. I could not have constructed a better exercise to teach her the benefits of relaxing, accepting and letting go.

During the last six months of Maddy's life, I had brought in a massage therapist and a cancer coach to be part of her support team. Both women were my friends and colleagues, and they did Maddy great good. She had grown much weaker, had lost considerable weight, and needed to sleep more. Our sessions together became simpler, less demanding, and focused mostly on supporting deep relaxation with music and reading aloud from books on the possibility of afterlife (her request). Maddy had once told me that she had never been to a spa, and it was something she hoped to do before she died. So my therapist friends and I decided to propose to Maddy a spa experience which would be held at my home in the country. I would have access to my grand piano, Heide would set up her massage table in front of the big windows that looked upon the mountains, and Ellen would arrange for a simple lunch of healthy foods. We would gently transport Maddy to and from, and keep the excursion brief enough so that it wouldn't tire her excessively, but long enough so she could enjoy herself. Maddy did not hesitate in accepting our invitation. In fact, she was delighted and looked forward to it with happiness.

We were all well aware of Maddy's frailty, and I must say that I was concerned that all might not go well. But the adventure was a success, given the supreme awareness and sensitivity of my team, and Maddy's determination to let us help her in every way. She even suggested that we "take a little walk" out to the woods next to the house, so she could smell the trees and hear the birds one more time. We kept her sturdy as she took a dozen or so steps into the trees, and then we all stood together and listened to the pulse of nature on a late spring day. Maddy knew her limit and told us it was time to go back home. It had been a full and wonderful day, the last time she was to leave the nursing home, the last time she was ever to be outside.

A few weeks later, her final decline set in. I spent our last visits singing softly at her bedside, always leaving her favorite CDs and tapes available so the nurses could play them as she requested.

She had made it clear to her family that her final visits with them were done, she was ready to say goodbye, and that she wanted only her boyfriend Barney present at the end. I missed Maddy's death, and I regret that. Perhaps some breathing and toning support might have eased her passing. But we can never know the exact time of death, and I have missed many. In her last hour, still conscious but groggy from pain medications, she asked Barney to move her from her bed to the reclining chair, where they cuddled together. Barney later told me that she had seemed agitated, wanted to move around, a behavior I have often seen when the dying are desperately trying to get out of their bodies. As he held her in the chair, she called out for the nurse, and then she died.

I will never know just what Maddy was feeling in her last moments. I suspect it wasn't pure relaxation, acceptance and a full readiness to let go. But I do know that this brave and truly loveable woman had done everything she could to prepare herself for finally giving up control and finding release. All that effort had helped her down a long road, and surely must have helped at the very end.

I'll end this chapter on difficult emotions with a story of a very brief encounter I had with a family at the hospital where I currently work. I was just finishing up with a patient when a nurse approached me and said, "There's a woman being transferred by ambulance to our unit from Dartmouth Hitchcock, as we speak. Her primary diagnosis is COPD (a serious pulmonary disease), but she's dying and wants to be here in the Garden Room (our hospital's suite for dying patients and families) where she's close to home. Sounds like the family is a pretty tough bunch. Very angry and hostile, caused a lot of trouble down there. They'll be on their way here, not far behind the ambulance."

Unknown to us at the time, there were actually 15 family members, ten enraged adults and five small children, about to crash through the doors of our little community hospital. An hour later,

Mom (the patient) arrived first, and the nurse and I got to work, settling her down in the suite. She was exhausted from travel, struggling to breathe, and looked stunned and anxious. For the next 45 minutes, we worked quietly together, the nurse with technical matters, I sitting next to our patient, holding her hand, talking in soothing tones, and finally singing her to sleep. She was comfortable, and this phase of our work was complete. But we both knew a herd of raging relatives was about to barge in and disrupt everything.

I left the suite and stood lookout in the hallway until I saw her family striding toward me in the distance. I rushed back to the patient's room, alerted the nurse, and thinking very quickly on my feet, asked that she just continue what she was doing and trust me. I picked up my medicine drum, stood by the bedside, and began to sing a lovely old American folk hymn, "How Can I Keep From Singing?" In the middle of the second phrase, the door abruptly opened and the eldest son appeared, looking like he was ready to fight. As soon as he stepped into the room and perceived the peaceful scenario being enacted, the angry contortions on his face melted away and he approached his mother with tears in his eyes. As each new unfriendly face appeared behind him, I looked into their eyes as I sang, and the fury turned into tears. In a minute's time, we had created together a roomful of weeping adults and questioning but quieting children, all gathered around their matriarch's bedside as she slept. A difficult and potentially dangerous situation had been defused, by the calm energies of a nurse and therapist working together, and of course, by the music.

I was reminded that evening of how the difficult emotion of anger is so often a substitute for other deeper emotion that is not as easy to access. This family was undoubtedly accustomed to using aggression when feeling vulnerable, when fear and deep sadness was what they were truly feeling. The transformation I witnessed was not that unusual. I've been party to this kind of healing magic many times, although I'll admit that these folks began from an unusually volatile place. The distance their hearts traveled the moment they entered that room, full of peaceful energy and the loveliness of music, was vast. From anger and fear, to love and grief—just where they needed to be.

Six

Music is a Visual Art

"Gesture and music are alike in that they have powers of extension
beyond known measurements."

Robert Henri, 1960

Every Thursday afternoon I meet with a delightful group of elders
at the extended care nursing facility attached to the hospital where
I currently work. These folks are not actively dying, but they are
generally in the final phase of their lives. Many are psychologically
shrouded by the effects of advanced dementia, a few are still mentally
alert but physically disabled and weakened by old age and various
disease processes. Within the secret chambers of their hearts, all
would wish to be living "at home," but this home away from home,
an award-winning healthcare facility, is by far the very best option
available to them in central Vermont. They are lovingly cared for
in a comfortable, clean and lovely setting by a staff of remarkable
people who treat them all like family.

We meet around a piano in a large, light-filled common room,
warmly decorated with comfortable sofas and rocking chairs. In a
place of honor, at one end of the room, is a wonderful free-standing
Victorian music box which plays old-fashioned brass discs of
favorite songs. Just before 3 p.m., a dozen or more residents are
set around the piano in their wheelchairs, often joined by family
members or other visitors, to listen to an hour of piano music and
song. We re-enact their memories of the old days of childhood,

when many of them gathered with their families in the parlors of their farmstead homes to listen to mothers, aunts or sisters play the old upright piano. They remember singing old hymns or the popular songs of the early twentieth century together, usually on Sunday evenings when the hard work of the week was behind them. "In the Shade of the Old Apple Tree" was sung then, and is sung again today at these sessions. We keep it very informal, allowing for reminiscing and storytelling in between musical pieces. Those who can, join in. And those who have lost the ability to speak or sing, simply listen, sleep, or express their feelings with body movement and facial expression. It is often a joyous, sometimes a poignant and sad, time of sharing that has brought us all, residents, visitors and staff alike, closer together, just like those simple family musical gatherings of yore.

Recently I was playing the ragtime piano music of Scott Joplin, launching into a little talk about its origins, when an elder lady recalled hearing one of her aunts playing this music at the old movie theater in town. Aunt Nellie was the piano player who accompanied the silent films that came to town before 1929, during the earliest days of cinema when all was black and white, and the technical apparatus for sound had not yet been developed. It was the pianist's job to add a live soundtrack to the film as the storyline progressed, adapting the music to the action and mood and emotion as necessary. As a pianist myself, I can't imagine a more demanding musical job, especially if it was done well. Some of these players played "by ear," improvising as they went along. Others must have been better trained, adapting actual piano pieces, some classical, others popular, to the requirements of the tale. But there wasn't any time for a break. I suppose the only reprieve was that the duration of these old films was not as long as modern films. Aunt Nellie must have truly earned the meager pay she made at this job. As the elder described it, she and her little friends sat on hard benches in the small, dark, wood-framed theater which still stands in the center of town today, complete with its original marquee. She remembered how the music her aunt played carried them through the thrills and spills of action-packed stories, heightening their emotions and coloring the moving images in a way that offered them the best fun of the week. Without her aunt's music, it would have been a very different, lifeless experience indeed.

During my leisure time at home, I like nothing better than lying back in the recliner covered in a lap blanket and watching a good film. My sensitive ears usually tune in to the musical soundtrack pretty early on, especially if the music is effective and interesting. Musical scores by Mark Isham, Phillip Glass and Arvo Part make for an unusual and interesting experience. But classical music applied to beautiful visuals can carry me through a heightened sensory experience that often stays with me for many hours, even days. Films that feature the popular music of my youth, Simon and Garfunkel, Cat Stevens, 1950s rock 'n roll, the Rolling Stones (there was so much great music then!) carry me back to the physical and emotional thrill of that time.

Susanne Langer, the late aesthetic philosopher, wrote "Music is a wordlessly presented conception of what life *feels* like" [my italics] (Langer, 1957, pp.59–60). Music can easily add more color, energy and emotion to something we are seeing. It emphasizes and strengthens the lifelike experience of watching a moving picture. But I am not only talking about what we see with our "outer eyes." We also have "inner eyes" that can see the images and moving pictures of our memories, dreams and imaginations. When one is dying, or living out the final stage of life and preparing for death, the inner eye can be awakened by the musical experience, revealing worlds of particular, personal meaning. As the importance of the outer world begins to wane, a door to an inner world can be opened, offering wondrous places to explore, enjoy and settle within.

I met Rosie when she was 77 years old, caring for her husband who was veering down the slippery road of dementia. She herself was not yet a hospice patient, but she was eligible for palliative care related to her own medical issues. Rosie had a blood platelet disorder called thrombocytopenia, as well as a bowel obstruction caused by intestinal cancers slowly growing in her body. She was also legally blind, virtually without sight since childhood, most likely the result of measles infection. Despite her blindness, Rosie was highly functional, went about her household duties easily, cleaned her own colostomy bag, and rarely complained about her physical ailments.

Like many older country women in Vermont who grew up on dairy farms, she was warm-hearted but tough-minded, and accepted and adapted to whatever life dished out. She was prone to some anxiety and sleeplessness, however. So I was sent to her aid.

Rosie told me that she loved music, especially gentle classical and Celtic music. Her favorite instrument was the harp. She told me a childhood story about how she and her brother would play the old pump organ in the parlor of their home. Her brother, stricken by polio, didn't have the use of his legs, so he would sit on the bench and play the keyboard while Rosie stooped down underneath and pushed the pumping pedals with both hands. I loved the image of two physically disabled children cooperating to make music. She had been very close to her brother, and despite their disabilities, they always played together outside, roaming the woods and fields surrounding the farmhouse, helping each other along the way.

One day Rosie asked me why she still was able to see in her dreams, even though she was blind. She added that sometimes she even dreamed in color. It was an important question for her to ask. I told her that she still had the use of her "inner eyes," even though her outer eyes had been damaged. When she slept and dreamed at night, her inner eyes opened and revealed a world separate from the outer world we live in, but no less real. I suggested that if she exercised her inner eyes more often, *that* sight might become even more vivid. Would she like to use music and a guided exercise to see what her inner eyes might see? Rosie was always enthusiastic about my suggestions, so the following week we ventured outdoors to a grassy knoll close to the house, with CD player in hand and a pretty quilt to sit on.

It was a lovely early summer day, just warm enough. We sat under the shade of a maple tree, refreshed by a light breeze bearing sweet scents of new grass and early flowering plants. I turned on the music, a slow movement from Mozart's Harp Concerto, and guided Rosie through a deep breathing exercise I had already taught her (to help with her sleeplessness and anxiety). It struck me how keenly she seemed to be enjoying the sensory experience of just being outside; how receptive her senses of smell and touch and hearing must be after all these years of blindness. I then asked her to close her eyes and imagine herself walking down a woodland path, following its twists and turns, taking in every sensory effect along the way, including the visual. I encouraged her to follow the path until she reached a place of special comfort and importance to her. I told her I would now leave her to explore and experience her special place, while we both simply listened to the beautiful music. As the movement was coming to a close, several minutes later, I gently guided Rosie back to the quilt under the maple tree, and asked her to open her eyes.

Rosie was very excited and happy about the "movie" that she saw. She reported walking along a familiar cow-path from her childhood days. She described the trees, the ground, the smells of the pine needles, all in clear detail. The path rose to a favorite white birch stand that she loved. When she looked across the valley from the highest point in the path she saw two neighbors working in their field. She saw her "Papa" several times. Then she came upon what she called the waterworks, a clear, cold spring where her polio-stricken brother engineered a simple pipe system. It was a place they often went to together. She was absolutely surprised at what she saw, and just how vivid and real it seemed. It was a scene, a motion picture if you will, of things she hadn't remembered for many years, and it brought her great comfort and joy. Rosie learned that day just how keen her inner sight was, and that she could visit these beloved places whenever she relaxed, put on her favorite calming music, and asked her inner eyes to bring her there.

No tale is sadder than the loss of a young parent. Unlike Rosie, who lived another two years, and who from her lofty perch of 80 years had found satisfaction and joy in raising a son to adulthood, watched him reach the maturity of mid-life, and also enjoyed the early years of grandchildren, a young parent's job of nurturing the next generations is sometimes cut short by disease and finally death. Although the loss of a *child* to death is devastatingly difficult, I think the loss of a young *parent* is unspeakably painful for the young family he or she must leave behind, most especially the children.

I met Kathy just two months before the end of her life. We had limited time together, only four music therapy sessions, but this brave young woman made the most of the various kinds of support my hospice team offered her and her family. She was 40 years old, declining rapidly from aggressive metastatic melanoma, a deadly cancer that begins as a lesion on the skin, but often spreads very quickly to internal organs. She hadn't had much time to process the inevitability of her death, and she was frightened and despairing. She and her husband, Dan, had two growing children, a 14-year-old daughter and 12-year-old son. This family was in a state of shock and anxiety, made all the more overwhelming by the fact that things were moving along at breakneck speed, from diagnosis to end of life.

Fortunately, the emotional needs of Kathy's husband and children were being addressed by one of my esteemed colleagues, an art and bereavement counselor who specializes in work with children. I could breathe a bit easier knowing that they were in good hands, giving me the focus I needed to support Kathy, who was facing not only the loss of her own shortened life, but the loss of two young children who still needed her desperately. How one comes to accept this kind of cruel reality and then let go is beyond my understanding. I didn't know if it would be possible for this young mother to reach any degree of acceptance and peace with this situation. Even though Kathy knew all the facts about her medical condition, had been told by her doctor that nothing more could be done to save her life, that death would come soon, she stated vehemently, "I'm gonna fight this thing," as if not only her's but her children's lives depended on it. A good mother will fight until the end, but battling down the path toward her last breath was not going to make things easier on anyone, most especially Kathy. We had some work to do together.

Kathy had always enjoyed music. She had many recordings of favorite popular artists, and before her illness had enjoyed spending time not just listening, but singing along with abandon. I encouraged her to continue to do this, even though she was beginning to weaken. She had time alone at home while her kids were at school and Dan was working, giving her the privacy she needed to belt out a song or two. But even though she tried, she sadly confessed that she could no longer do it; that looking for the old joy of singing made her feel guilty. How could she open herself up to one iota of joy when her children were suffering so? And would continue to suffer long beyond her remaining time here. We would have to use music for another, different purpose.

One day Kathy told me that the social worker on the hospice team and I were the only two people she could share deep confidences with. She told me how some of her extended family members and friends really didn't know how to help her, despite their good intentions. She recognized the difference between a calm, strong person who would simply listen to her, and being bombarded with frantic "help" that missed the mark, and served only to make the helper feel better. It seemed that many people were swarming around this family in need, not understanding how to truly help, and creating much more stress than was already built into the situation. What Kathy really needed was good time with her little family, some assurance that her husband and children would be well supported beyond her death, and a "vacation" from all the drama that many in her larger circle were creating.

I suggested we try listening to some special, dreamy music I had brought along, while I guided her through a relaxation exercise and an imaginary journey to find her safe place. Kathy somehow was able to trust me easily, despite our brief association, always expressing confidence that what I offered might help her. It was a sign of her great inner strength, as well as her desperate need for something that would carry her through this nightmare, that she remained open to things that she had probably never contemplated practicing before her illness. She gave me the great gift of turning herself over to my care. Thankfully, our work together did bring her some benefit, and the kind of compassionate help she truly deserved.

By this time, Kathy was bound in a hospital bed which was located in a sunny three-season porch attached to the rear of the house. She could no longer carry out her practical role as mother and wife, depending upon Dan and her children to work together on household chores. With little else that she could still do, taking an imaginary "vacation" was perfect for this time. So I put on the music CD: lilting flutes, acoustic guitar, simple piano. She followed my instruction to lay back upon her pillows, close her eyes, and to breathe in deeply through her nose on my count of four, then exhale through her mouth on my slow count of six. She settled into this gentle rhythm of cleansing breath, as I continued: "Now Kathy, I'd like you to imagine that you are hiking along a mountain trail. You are alone, your body feels strong and able, and you are enjoying the freshness of the day, the blue of the sky above. Notice what you are wearing…pay attention to the sounds that surround you…feel the ground under your feet…take in the scents as you continue to breathe in deeply, followed by the sensation of letting the breath go. Take your time to stop and look around…and then continue on your way. Let's see where you end up. Allow yourself to anticipate arriving at a place that will fill you with wonder, a beautiful place that will feel very peaceful and safe. When you get there, you will recognize it as your special, safe place. Again, take your time investigating this place, find a comfortable spot upon which to sit and look and take it all in. I will be quiet for the next several minutes while you do this. Then I will return and guide you back. Enjoy yourself."

After Kathy returned to full awareness of the sunroom with eyes open, her facial expression was soft and calm. I kept the lovely music playing while she described what she saw, where she went: "I found myself in a courtyard surrounded by big, white, stone buildings. The buildings were decorated and held up with massive columns, they were very majestic. It was quiet, no one else was there but me. I found a stone bench and rested there for awhile. There were some gardens around, but mostly it was a place all white and light. I *did* feel safe there. It was wonderful."

When I have guided others in this exercise, often the safe place they discover is a natural setting: a beach, a meadow, a forest, a mountaintop. Sometimes it is a favorite room, the backyard of a deceased grandmother, a comfy chair next to a fireplace. Kathy's scene was unusual for its hardness, its massive solidity. And yet, given her dire straits, it seemed perfectly suited to meeting her need for something solid and strong to hold on to. This place of hard rock and fortress-like construction helped her feel safe, protected, and ultimately peaceful.

During the final few weeks of her life, Kathy repeated this exercise, with or without me, whenever she became afraid or overwhelmed. This practice helped her to make some decisions about safeguarding her privacy by limiting friend and extended family visits. She also drew her children into a special quilt-making project, something they could do together even while she rested in bed. At this time, as she was forced to let go of so many precious things and people in her life, Kathy found a way to take back a little control in an uncontrollable situation. I shall always admire her for "fighting" for all the right stuff in the end: safety, connection and peace.

The imagination coupled with our inner visual aptitude can be a vital resource, even as other bodily functions weaken at end of life. In her book, *Imagery and Healing: Shamanism and Modern Medicine*, Jeanne Achterberg writes, "The shamans claim to be able to enter at will an unusual state of consciousness, one conducive to special *problem-solving* abilities… It is a dream-like state, somewhere between sleep and wakefulness, where vivid imagery experiences are possible" [my italics] (Achterberg, 1985, p.23). I have found that ordinary people, while supported by resonant vocal/verbal guidance, along with appropriate music as background sound (as described in Rosie's and Kathy's stories), can have mini-shamanic experiences which help them solve particular problems at end of life.

Dorian was a 94-year-old gentlewoman, very bright and alert, well educated and still enjoying her life of reading. She had taught French and Latin in schools for many years, and especially enjoyed our music therapy visits in the private care home where she had recently settled. She remained quite functional until the final few weeks of her life six months later, when she died peacefully in her sleep from end-stage cardiac disease. Dorian favored hearing me sing some of the old Christian hymns, as well as the ancient Latin chants of Hildegard of Bingen. Her mother had died in the flu epidemic of 1918, when Dorian was seven years old. She was raised by her aunt Amy, and my singing prompted her to remember the times she accompanied her uncle on the piano, as he sang these old hymns long ago.

Dorian was always thoughtful in her speech. One day she said, "I love listening to all this talent… You sound like a priest… I wonder why I am still here." As our relationship deepened, she confided that she never spoke directly with her son or other family members about her coming death. She said she didn't want to upset them. So she talked with me instead, telling me her particular wishes for funeral and special music, hoping that I would pass the information along. Of course, I was honored to help her with this simple request.

At our final visit, seven days before she died, I noted that Dorian was weaker, no longer able to sit in her chair for long periods of time. As was our custom, I sang a collection of songs while she rested, ending with a few hymns. We sat companionably together for a few moments, enjoying the peaceful quiet that follows a beautiful melody. Then Dorian spoke: "You know, I never learned how to swim. So many of these old hymns are about the river we have to cross when we die. I wonder, will I be able to make it to the other side if I can't swim?" We both chuckled a little, but her question was asked in earnest. So I responded, "Dorian, why don't we practice getting you across right now? I'll sing another river hymn after I guide you to the edge and then into the water. I think you can do it in your imagination." So this gentlewoman closed her eyes and followed my lead, as I sang one of the loveliest Black spirituals:

> "Deep River, my home is over Jordan
> Deep River, Lord, I want to cross over into campground.
> Oh, don't you want to go to that gospel feast,
> That promised land where all is peace?
> Deep River, my home is over Jordan
> Deep River, Lord, I want to cross over into campground."

(Anonymous, arr. Harry Burleigh, Ricordi and Co., 1917)

I sang it through three times, to give Dorian a chance to swim to the other side. When she opened her eyes, she smiled and said: "I made it. I didn't swim like Esther Williams, but I made it!" (Esther Williams was a famous American swimmer and movie star in the 1940s and 50s.) Our imaginations speak in metaphor and symbol of deeper doubts and fears that may keep us from moving forward. By seeing herself take on the challenge of swimming across the water, Dorian found the inner assurance she needed for the big transition ahead. When I received a call a week later informing me of her passing during the night, I imagined her speeding across that river, executing an elegant Australian crawl.

There are occasions when I am asked to give a presentation or lead a workshop on the work that I do. When facilitating groups, I often end the experience with a music listening exercise that is designed to elicit visual imagery and stimulate creativity. I call this exercise "Sound Gathering" because of the way it supports people to take in, to "gather" the music, and then watch its effects. I also like to think of groups of people as "gatherings." You will see, as we go through the exercise, that "gathering" comes into play on several levels. The process ends with the creation of a poem, collectively written by members of the gathering and myself.

Let me take you through it...

Imagine yourself seated in a circle with 20 people or so. I lower the lights and ask each of you to close your eyes, to find a comfortable way of sitting on your chair with both feet planted on the floor. I guide you into a relaxation response with deep breathing and muscle relaxation techniques. I then play a piece of music, either on CD or live piano, something that has been specially selected for this group, usually five to seven minutes in duration. For this occasion, I choose Ottorino Respighi's final movement from the *Botticelli Triptych*, titled "La Nascita di Venere" (Birth of Venus). Before the music begins, I instruct each of you to pay close attention to any visual imagery that may appear via your inner eye. If you see nothing, that's fine. You may want to notice if certain emotions or memories are aroused, or if any physical changes in your body state occur. Then we listen.

So now, the music has ended and I gently guide you back into the room, ask you to open your eyes, and then follow with another instruction: would you please now write down (on the scrap of paper I provided before we began), in a sentence, a simple phrase, or individual words, what it was that you experienced. Please be as descriptive as possible. Take your time as you review your inner journey. After each has completed this task, I invite each person to speak in turn, around the circle, the words that they wrote. I encourage them to breathe in deeply before they speak, and to let the sound of their voice ring out to the others. This way of "giving voice" is like making an offering to the gathering, where the vocal sounds are all gathered together in the center of the circle.

This exercise could easily end here, but we take it another step further. I gather up all the scraps of paper, bring them home, cut out each prominent and descriptive word, and set all the words out on my table. I shuffle them around and keep them there for a few days after I've looked at each of them. When I feel ready, I sit down and begin piecing together a poem from all this raw material. This part of the process is very intuitive and fun for me. I never know what will emerge from this creative process, which is certainly not just my own, but nourished by all the creative imagery and sensation of the gathering members. After the poem feels complete, I make copies and send them out to all the participants of the workshop. I imagine that the poem has a very different meaning for each of them.

As I reread each of the poems that I've collected in this way through the years, I notice that the themes of life and death, loss and longing, gratitude and awe reappear, even though the participants in these workshops are healthy people, engaged and active, perhaps many years from their ends of life. Despite that, it seems that we carry within us a deep yearning to understand why we are here, where we are going. Don Juan, the Yaqui sorcerer in Carlos Castaneda's books, taught that death always walks with us on our left side, like a shadow following us wherever we go. We may not consciously mull over the big mysteries each day of our busy lives, but I suspect that somewhere deep inside each of us, that brew simmers. Let's end this chapter with a favorite sound gathering poem of mine. What meanings might it have for you?

"Go down to the bass notes
and listen to the tinkling of your skin.
What would it cost you to let the white moonlight
fall on your long life?
The smiling loon understands your sleepy nature,
how you get lost in the ebb of each magnetic evening.
Walking slowly to another beginning,
you touch the new baby, featherweight.
You both are babbling in tongues.
Can you see yourself weaving and dancing
toward your funeral boat,
while a soft rain whispers, over and over,
'I have loved you all my life?'
Let it whisk you away and release you
to Home."

(Runningdeer, 2009)

Seven

The Disabled and Mentally Ill

"Beauty is itself a cure for psychological malaise."

James Hillman, 1996

Many years ago I played a benefit concert with a few musician friends for a woman who needed help with mounting medical bills. It was a community affair where many people, with various skills, contributed to the effort. The poster art was created by a young fellow with autism, and I've kept it hanging on my wall all these years as a reminder of how strange we musician-creatures are, indeed how strange perhaps we all are. The scene is of three monkey-people playing chamber music: a pianist, a flutist and a violinist. The colors are vivid, and there is a motion in the picture that suggests the flow of an unusual brand of wacky music. I love it. It's a reminder of how the musical part of me is indeed free of a conventional, normal mindset; that music is where I can safely express all my eccentricity, intimidating depth, otherworldliness... and perhaps a bit of madness.

As I bring music to the dying, I imagine an aura of *my* strangeness following me into those settings, inviting others to feel more comfortable settling into personal terrain that is not the daily norm for *them*. Music mines our depths and free expression, however strange, at a time when we are witness to an extraordinary process.

But the benign "madwoman" in me has found no more comfortable place than when assisting those who are mentally ill or disabled. Sharing music with these poor souls who have suffered a lot while living, and who now face the end of their days here, has been a special privilege, one that has brought me closer to my own true nature.

Phillip was by far the most eccentric and delightfully "mad" patient I've ever encountered. When we met, he was 70 years old, living with and caring for his wife who had multiple sclerosis. *She* was actually my hospice patient, and has a separate story of her own, but it's Phillip's story I want to tell. Throughout his life, Phillip had had mental health problems, manic-depression and possible obsessive-compulsive disorder. His conditions had been managed with medication, so he was able to function reasonably well, and had proved his capabilities as primary caregiver for his wife during the last few years of her life. When we met, wife Lois needed 24-hour care, and Phillip had learned how to use medical technologies to feed her, keep her clean and comfortable, and provide her with a safe home-base. The hospice team supplemented his care, and things went pretty well until her death three years later. This was one of those cases where I had lots of time to acquaint myself with a patient and her spouse. We three developed a very warm relationship, and two years after Lois died, when Phillip himself became our hospice patient, I was well poised to assist him through his own dying process.

I don't know what Phillip's IQ was, but I'd bet that he was bordering on genius. He was incredibly inquisitive, knowledgeable and creative. I loved his childlike excitability when his mind grasped upon something novel. He played the piano, composed music, painted, created a "letter shorthand" system (his own language), always seemed to have a little project blooming on his desk. He loved the fact that I was an accomplished pianist, and turned his piano over to me each time I visited, so he and Lois could sit and listen to Chopin, Rachmaninoff (his two favorites), and a whole host of other composers. Lois's disease did not allow her to speak more than a couple of words, but Phillip verbalized their delight and enjoyment with giddy eloquence. Phillip's digital piano had a recording component, and after our first few sessions, he asked if we could record what I played so he and Lois could listen whenever they wished. One day, he exclaimed, "On New Year's Day, Lois and I listened to all the recordings three times!" I thought, "Poor Lois." But then reconsidered. I should mention that Phillip's wife was an ex-Catholic nun and had the demeanor of a saint. These two unusual people were devoted to each other, and she probably would have listened to the music over and over again, if it satisfied Phillip.

One day Phillip presented me with a CD copy of 41 miniature piano pieces he had written. He had become comfortable sharing his creative ideas and insights with me, and his original music gave me a glimpse of Phillip's inner self and how he perceived his world. Each little piece was no more than 60 seconds in duration, and their titles were both charming and funny: "Skipping," "Clarification," "The Oddballs," "The Headache," "The Little Lie," "Soaring," "Confusion," "Funeral March," "The Murk," "Doubts," "More Doubts," "I Dreamed." I was reminded of Bela Bartok's miniature piano pieces, some written for children, which also had names that encapsulated a feeling, a brief vision or experience. The form of Phillip's music was simple, like his own innocent nature, but the tonal colors, occasional dissonances and unruly, ear-catching counterpoint revealed an undercurrent of disturbance and strangeness that made Phillip one of a kind. With Phillip, I could laugh and play like a child, while switching back into a highly intellectual conversation about music history. *His* way of being enhanced *my* way of being. The circle of creative, slightly mad energy we shared with each other was healing for both of us. In a note written to accompany the CD, Phillip wrote: "Enclosed is a good CD of 'My Works'—though it is not jacketed properly and enclosed in a proper jewel case." Jewels, indeed.

As Phillip himself lay dying in a care home a few years later, I jumped back into his life with music at his deathbed. His close family of surviving siblings, nieces and nephews sat vigil and asked me to play Rachmaninoff on Phillip's piano, which had been moved to his bedside. It was clear, after finally meeting his relatives after all these years, that Uncle Phillip was a treasured member of the family, that he had been loved for his dear, quirky nature, and would be sorely missed. I felt the same way.

Willy's story breaks my heart. It wasn't as much his death that makes me sad, as the trials of his life. Willy was a 36-year-old man with the mental capacity of an eight-year-old boy. He was a full six feet tall with a stocky body, a blond crewcut and a lumbering gait. He lived alone in a small apartment in a town where he could easily walk to services and activities, vigilantly looked after by his parents who lived a short distance away, and well supported by county services for the mentally disabled. Willy had leukemia, and became a palliative care patient of ours during the final ten months of his short life. He was cared for by a local oncologist who would not give up on trying to save his life, so difficult is it to let go of the young. So Willy underwent chemotherapy treatments and numerous hospitalizations during our time together. He hated going to the hospital, where he couldn't get to go outside (like any other eight-year-old boy), and where he was terribly bored. I worked this case with my assistant grad student intern, who brought her guitar and drums and mellow voice to our music sessions, adding just the right touch for this young man/boy who loved the music of Phil Collins and the Bee Gees.

Willy had a problem with aggression. When he felt threatened and scared, he sometimes lashed out physically, creating public scenes that startled and scared those around him. Once, while feeling frustrated and angry in a grocery store, he upended a table of birthday cakes, creating quite a mess and lots of havoc. But like the truly innocent little boy that he was, he always felt tremendous remorse after these episodes, crying out his apologies and sorrow. Willy was afraid of his own powerful feelings, didn't know how to restrain his big body, and got himself into trouble.

Willy called us "the music ladies," and beamed his bright smile when we visited. He loved showing us his vast train and truck collection. His trains were his special passion. Visiting a nearby train museum and the local hobby shops was a favorite pastime, often shared with his dad. So we sang songs about trains, veering into Woody Guthrie territory and away from his personal taste for more current popular music. Though Willy's attention span was limited, he accepted our music politely and then kept us up to date on what was going on for him. Unlike so many of us "normal" people, Willy had no self-consciousness about baring his soul. He was always the one to launch into a discussion of his feelings, his daily challenges, the simple things that made him happy, the stuff that scared him silly in the night.

I hoped to help Willy understand and accept his own power, to learn how to channel it in better ways. We brought three large drums one day and encouraged him to play some simple rhythms with us. But he was reluctant to strike the drumhead with any force, so tentative and afraid was he of his own strength. He feared that he might break it, even though we assured him that it was tough and ready for his strength. From time to time, we brought out the drums again, and eventually Willy was able to join in and play without the same fear. The very best drum session occurred while Willy was telling us his current story, not paying much mind to what his strong hands were doing. He surprised himself that day, with how easily he was able to channel some of his physical strength, in a good way.

I understood Willy's fear of his own energy as his attempt to control deep and sometimes frightening passions. He was, after all, a 36-year-old man with a strong body, one that most likely had never enjoyed the release of sexual activity. He was a lonely guy who had trouble making friends, and who carried around a deep sadness and remorse for his occasional anti-social behavior. Somehow he understood the emotional and physical burden that was carried by his own parents, and he felt badly whenever his mother had to come over to wash his dishes for him. He was a man with life-threatening leukemia, who was able to understand the ramifications of this only with his eight-year-old mind. No wonder he felt anxious in bed at night, and became elated whenever a friendly visitor showed up. These were the parts of Willy's life story that broke my heart.

One day, Willy said he'd like us to listen to one of his favorite songs by Phil Collins. He was oddly quiet and serious this day, and Willa and I respectfully watched as he placed a CD in the player and sunk to the floor a little distance away from us, in the privacy of his own thoughts and feelings. We all listened together to "Thru These Walls," a tender song about loneliness.

The lyrics create the scene of a child looking out his window, watching other boys and girls playing together. He hears their happy sounds muffled by the window glass and sees them having fun. But they are just beyond reach; he cannot join in. He wonders if they would invite him, if he would promise not to touch, not to cause any trouble. It is such a sad song of alienation, it made me wonder just what kind of childhood a great celebrity like Collins might have had to be able to express the same kind of pain and yearning for friendship that dear Willy lived with.

As the song ended, Willy remained motionless and thoughtful, and so did we. Intern Willa tried to draw him out a bit, thinking that Willy might need to talk about his own loneliness. But for Willy, that wasn't needed. I believe he just wanted to share his feelings with us through the song, nothing more. It was a lovely and poignant breakthrough for this fellow who had so feared his deep feeling, and how he might hurt others with it. His sharing that day was such a *gentle* and true expression.

This dear fellow finally ended up in the hospital for the last time, never to return home. As he lay dying, his devoted, bereft parents and I sat at his bedside. I played peaceful, mildly rhythmic music on his CD player as I guided Willy on a happy train ride through the countryside, speaking close to his ear. As we felt the mesmerizing pulsing clang of the rails together, Willy raised his arms weakly above his body and kept beat with his hands. He fell into a deep sleep soon after and died the following day.

At his wake, streams of people stopped by to pay their respects. As I embraced his mother, she said: "I never knew there were so many people in my son's life." During his daily walks through town, Willy had greeted many folks on the street, and he had left an impression, one that compelled them to remember him with warmth and sadness. His parents were held in the arms of a friendly community that day, as we all said goodbye to sweet Willy.

Both Willy and Phil struggled with mental illness or disability that presented substantial challenges as they lived and died. But there is another group of people who are so locked within frail bodies and broken minds that direct communication, especially meaningful verbal communication, is very difficult or impossible. These people, like all the rest of us, go through the dying process too. Supporting them in this transit requires different ways of communication. Music can reach these folks beautifully, so I was often called in to a residential facility which serves the most severely physically and mentally disabled population in our county. This modest home, perched on a hillside in Barre, provides 24-hour intensive care to those who are living with serious birth defects, brain damage, severe Down's syndrome and other pervasive mental disabilities. These people, unlike Willy or Phil, cannot live independently at all. They depend upon medical staff for tube feedings, for general hygiene, for technical help with breathing and being moved. The more able among them are sometimes driven in a van to local destinations so they can get out and see a tiny bit of the world. But for the most part, they spend their time in bed, or in their chairs, watching TV or staring into space. It is difficult at first to encounter this way of living. But after I'd worked with a few residents during their ends of life, and learned how to include the whole residential family in the musical experience, I came to cherish my time with these people.

This home serves no more than a dozen or so residents at a time. So gathering all in the central room, where many of them spent their day anyway, was an easy task. I brought an array of instruments with me on my visits: autoharp, hand drums, bells, dulcimer, harmonica. And eventually I arranged to have an old acoustic piano donated to the facility, so that I might play and sing all kinds of music. It wasn't the best of instruments, with its sticky action and inability to hold a good tuning, but I made the best of it, with the results I had hoped for. There's something about live music that audio just can't stand up to. For these folks, simply seeing someone play an instrument well while hearing the musical sounds and energy fill the room, was a great novelty and stimulation. Often people would be roused from sleep, or others would sleep more soundly, emitting loud snores of deep relaxation. Others would squeal with joy or wave their arms in response to the musical movement. The few who could still speak, albeit with great difficulty, would be enthralled as I fulfilled their requests: old Roy Rogers songs, Christmas carols, patriotic favorites, "O Susannah!," "Twinkle Twinkle Little Star." Some had no way at all to express a response, except perhaps with their eyes. But I, so many times, sensed their attention and focus, as I might sense the presence of night creatures in a dark forest, hidden but there.

Most of these people could hear, even though they might not be able to speak or move or swallow or understand the world around them in any way close to what we consider normal. And because of this, the music and sound that reached them was like a lifeline thrown out into a deep, lonely sea. Something shifted within these folks during music sessions, something I do not fully comprehend, and which they could never explain to me. But I trust that it was good.

If I had my way, these often forgotten people would have in their parlor the same kind of beautiful grand piano that I occasionally find in well-endowed hospitals or nursing homes. They would have a live music session every single day of their lives, providing them with a special kind of nourishment that feeds the soul, for soulful they are, without a doubt. As they die, as many of them do in youth or mid-life, gentle music and toning and breathing support would always be brought to their bedsides, along with massage, Reiki and spiritual support. It would be the right thing to do.

Eight

The Rich and the Poor

"Your fat king, and your lean beggar, is but variable service;
two dishes, but to one table.
That is the end."

Hamlet, William Shakespeare, Act IV, Scene 3

Each of us is born into socio-economic circumstances not of our own making. Some of us make gains on our origins through hard work, others are born into easy affluence and have no urgent need or desire to make alterations, still others are born into the world with little, and often die with even less. We see examples of diverse economic circumstances throughout Vermont, and I have seen the rich, the poor, and those who have just enough die in my care. The home settings of these deaths reflected with stark honesty all the economic differences among us, from the dark, squalid cabin in the woods to the palatial estate on the hill, the tidy ranch house in a 1950s development to the rusted trailer without running water. Despite the settings, however, one thing was always the same: someone living there was dying, and those who loved this person were suffering. Death is the great equalizer.

How human beings face the challenges of living and dying is indeed a measure of character. In the stories that follow, it mattered not if a family was rich or poor. What mattered was how both despair and devotion could coexist, in equal measure, in difficult circumstances. In the end, it is spiritual courage and love that override the importance of material resources. Therein lies our true wealth.

Once upon a time there were two middle-aged brothers who lived in a rented trailer just off "the strip" of malls, service stations and fast food stops that connects the Granite City with the state capital. The older brother, Gary, was dying of intestinal cancer which had metastasized to his lungs. The younger, Keith, developmentally disabled and with a speech impediment that strained verbal communication, was his brother's caregiver. Both men had served time in prisons, for crimes unknown to me. They were poor, and given Gary's declining health and inability to work, were dependent upon economic help from those of us taxpayers who find ourselves in much better conditions. When I met them three months before Gary's death, they were being threatened with eviction from their trailer home. These guys had seen pretty hard times, had looked after one another throughout their whole lives, more often with Gary watching out for Keith, before his serious illness put that to an end. Now the roles were reversed, and Keith had stepped up to the plate with courage and determination that he would take care of his older brother to the end. Like a mother caring for a sick child, Keith fed his brother, lifted him to the commode, changed his colostomy bag, gave him his medications, cleaned up after him when he vomited, all as best he could.

I had heard plenty of stories at staff meetings about the unkept and crowded conditions in the trailer, about the practical challenges of being able to keep Gary at home while he died, which was the family's wish. We on the hospice team were supplementing and coaching care to the best of our ability, and now it was my turn to be added to the mix. The day I met these folks, Gary was still able to be wheelchaired into the tiny livingroom, though it was clear that he tired easily. Brother Keith and a visiting sister joined us as I offered songs and simple explanations of how I'd like to bring music into their home as they walked down this treacherous road together. As always, I had read all the medical and social service documentation about this case beforehand. But what I discovered was missing in this record was the unmistakable sweetness and devotion of these two men. Indeed, "the meek shall inherit the earth." As I sang, Gary beamed and Keith cried. Their sister requested some Bible songs, since all three were members of a local fundamentalist Christian group. So I sang "Jesus Loves Me," "In the Garden," and "Amazing Grace," moving on to other kinds of music, Black spirituals, American folk tunes, Stephen Foster melodies— all of which was enthusiastically received. As Gary showed signs of tiring and I concluded the session, he said: "While you sang, I saw a vision of my mother on the wall. And then I heard a voice that said my time to go is near." I hearkened back to the words of "Amazing Grace:" "I once was blind, but now I see," suggesting that his nearness to death might be opening up new ways of seeing for him. Gary's willingness to share deep things with me, and all of us in the room, could not have surprised me more. Before meeting these two ex-convicts, my expectations had been radically different from what I actually found. There was such sweet, gentle love and authenticity here.

But there was also despair. Over time I realized just how much Keith had depended upon his older brother to protect and companion him. Knowing that his brother would be dying soon, leaving him to fend for himself, was a reality that troubled Keith and often left him feeling anxious and hopeless. During musical visits that followed, the bolstering effect they had on the younger brother was just as important as the calming effect they had on the older. Toward the end of Gary's life, when caring for him was no longer feasible at home, and he was transferred to a local nursing home, Keith and I spent hours together at the bedside, making and listening to songs. Keith would say, in his garbled enunciation, "You sing so good. When some people sing, I just want to run away. But you really cheer me up."

During Gary's final days, although sleepy and unable to speak, he would reach out to take my hand. I sometimes held his head in my hands as I sang, as brother Keith sat close by, tears streaming down his cheeks. Just the previous week, Gary had admitted that he felt afraid, afraid of not ever waking up again. So in between songs, I used a gentle tone of voice to reassure him, "There is nothing to fear, Gary. Just be still and let go when you are ready."

One day before Gary died, I arrived in his room to find a hospice volunteer sitting at his bedside. This young man was an American Buddhist monk who brought his prayers of compassion to the dying. When I entered the room he said, "Someone left some loud country music on the CD player, so I turned it down a little." I suggested we turn it off altogether, along with disconnecting the telephone line on the bedside table so the ringer would no longer startle Gary, who was clearly on his way. I then invited my Buddhist friend to join me in some simple, rhythmic chants that prompted one, long exhalation of relief from Gary's spent body. How ironic, I thought, to be chanting Buddhist mantras to this gentle man who had found solace in a fundamentalist Christian church. But I trust that Gary would not have minded a bit, for all that filled his dying room that day was the same sweetness and devotion that had been hallmarks of strength during his hard life. Although I cannot write, "and they all lived happily ever after," I can say that these two brothers showed me the very best of being human.

Set high on a hill in the countryside is a large, newly built house, designed with many windows to take in the local views. The driveway is long and winding, probably a bit of a nuisance during our icy winters. As I drove up to the parking area, I was reminded of a splendid coach road leading to a porte cochère, or a long, tree-lined promenade fronting a lovely plantation. It was just a narrow road cut into the hill, but I still felt the expectancy of something special at its end. The surrounding yard was yet to be landscaped, so the exterior was still pretty stark. It was when I entered the home that I experienced its true sumptuousness.

I was kindly greeted by a 70-ish-year-old woman, Michaela, the daughter of an elderly Jewish lady, Layah, who was in hospice care. Michaela, a recent widow, was the primary caregiver for her 97-year-old mother. Other family members, Michaela's siblings and their families, lived very close by, and visited often. The family was well known in the region, as its members were successful professionals in the medical field. Layah, the family matriarch, was a remarkable woman who had endured the atrocities of the pogroms in the Ukraine. As a newly married young couple, Layah and her husband barely managed to escape. They were starving refugees for four years, hiding in forests during the day and fleeing at night. After standing in a frozen river all night while being shot at by border guards, they miraculously crossed over into Romania to a displaced persons camp. Eventually, they were sponsored with steerage passage to Canada, arriving in Halifax in 1921. Layah and her husband lost most of their family in the Holocaust. Layah's 85-year-old mother in the Ukraine was rounded up by the Nazis, lifted up by her hair, thrown into a grave and buried alive.

In Canada, Layah and her husband started a new life, raising and educating their children in the ancient cultural traditions of their native heritage, enriching their lives with a love of learning and art, as well as a strong drive to excel and contribute to the well-being of society. Layah was respected and loved by the small Jewish community in the region. Many people, Jews and non-Jews alike, turned out to pray the Kaddish for her spirit on the day of her memorial service. Her husband had died many years earlier.

But this story is not as much about Layah, as it is about Michaela. The day I met Michaela, she guided me through her home to a sitting area off the kitchen. Along the way, my eyes feasted on the beauty of colorful thick rugs from the Far East, wonderful paintings on the walls, many unusual artifacts most likely gathered from travels around the world, and an old Steinway grand piano. Michaela's husband, a doctor, had died a few years previous to our meeting, a victim of melanoma. She had cared for him too, during his final months, and had had insufficient time to recover from the physical and emotional duress of that before she took her mother in. As she shared her story with me, it became clear that Michaela was still in deep mourning for her beloved husband, even as she was anticipating the coming loss of her dear mother.

The rich comfort and beauty within this home contrasted dramatically with the palpable sorrow I felt all around me. There were obviously few, if any, financial worries here. But the heaviness of loss permeated the environment, and left me with a sense of deprivation of joy and peace. Loss begets the remembering of other losses. It's like accumulating compound interest on a growing principal. The well of sorrows in a lifetime can be very deep, indeed, and each time we are faced with another big impending loss, memory of past losses floods in, along with all that old accompanying pain. As Michaela talked about the end of her mother's life, she recalled the time of her husband's dying, and of how so very much she missed him. The timing of multiple losses in our lives is sometimes pretty unmerciful. I have encountered families who have lost important loved ones at a relentless pace, sometimes as many as three or four deaths within just a few years. Oftentimes difficult bereavements can lead to illness, both physical and emotional, which in the most extreme cases may result in yet another death in the family, that of the bereaved. I have witnessed that event most often when the death of a spouse is just too much to bear, especially for the elderly. So, although I saw that Michaela was a strong woman with still much to live for, I worried that the burden of losing two such important people in her life, within such a short time span, might leave her totally drained and deeply wounded for some time.

After Michaela shared her story with me, I asked if I might play some classical piano music for her and her mother, whose room was just a short walk down the hall. We kept Layah's door wide open so she could hear the music too, while Michaela sat nearer to the piano. There were accomplished musicians in this family, and at one time the piano had been played regularly. But since Michaela's husband's death, it had remained virtually silent. Michaela, who played herself, had not felt like touching it in a very long while. It seemed to me that getting the piano to sing again might help bring a bit of lightness and joy into the house, as well as help Michaela and her mother feel all the feelings of their lives, past and present.

While I used the piano to good effect, at times I also sat by Layah's bedside to work more intimately with her. She was suffering with esophageal cancer and was plagued with chronic pain throughout her body. At 97 years old, she was exhausted from enduring a long cycle of gnawing pain, alternating with sickness from narcotic medication. We practiced deep breathing exercises while listening to soothing music CDs, followed by instruction in how to do this for herself while she was alone. One day, as she was nearing death, I felt a presence behind me as I guided Layah into deep relaxation, telling her that her days of pain were almost over. As I peeked over my shoulder, I saw Michaela and her brother, a surgeon who had flown in to be with the family, holding each other in the doorway, tears streaming down their faces.

It is over ten years now since my time with this family. Although I've seen Michaela at various community affairs during the years, we have never had an opportunity to talk privately, or at length, since Layah's death. I have wondered about the aftermath of this story, especially if and how Michaela has been able to move forward in her own life. I needed to know how this special woman had navigated her course, so I arranged to meet her at her home to see and hear about how she was doing.

It was a gray, drizzly day, early autumn. I was anticipating the full harvest moon, due in 24 hours. The time of reaping. In my own life, I was feeling a fullness of good things. As Michaela greeted me at her door, I felt the warmth that I remembered well. But a new softness radiated from her, visible in the clear skin of her face, the glow in her eyes. As she led me to the sitting room off the kitchen, my senses were again enlivened by the rich beauty of her home, just as they had been a decade before. The old connection we had cultivated years ago was still strong, and we easily moved into sharing our stories.

Excusing the presence of her sewing machine on the dining table, Michaela explained that she was making hundreds of hand-crafted favors for her granddaughter's upcoming wedding. "She must be the granddaughter who was a little girl during your mother's end of life!" I exclaimed, noting the passage of time and all the changes it brings. Michaela went on to tell me about her grandchildren, their accomplishments, the exciting plans for a fall wedding, and just how proud she was of the lives her children and grandchildren were making for themselves. She explained that she would be boarding a plane in a few days to spend several weeks of wedding preparation with her younger family. Her face beamed, and I knew that she had safely made it through the darkest time of her bereavement because her descendants needed her love and attention. Giving herself over to them brought a good measure of joy into her life, and helped heal her heart.

I wondered aloud if she ever returned to playing the piano. She put out her arthritic hands and said, "No, I'll never be able to play like I used to. But others have played this piano, and there is music again in my home." She will always mourn and miss her husband and mother. She said, so poignantly, "They will always *not* be there, even though my well-meaning friends urge me to feel their presence." This is a sadness about absence that I believe has also softened her. It reminded me of "Distressed Haiku" written by the American Poet Laureate Donald Hall (2002):

> *"You think that their*
> *dying is the worst*
> *thing that could happen.*
>
> *Then they stay dead."*

We are all humbled and broken, made very small again, by the loss of those we have loved most. But when from that vulnerable state we are able to reach out and continue to love those in our midst, our spirits are strengthened, our humanity attains a new stature. We become more ourselves, innocent and true again.

Michaela is now well into her eighties. As she approaches her final years, she wears her heartbreak and joy like a glorious banner, symbol of the true riches of a long life. I applaud her.

Abject poverty—of material resources, of spirit, of joy—often leads to the final corruption and downfall of a person. I saw this happening in a squalid cabin in the woods to a man who lived there with his 43-year-old daughter, severely impaired by Down's syndrome and slowly dying of uterine cancer. Less than 12 months earlier, his wife had dropped dead on the floor of the cabin, leaving him to care for his disabled and terminally ill daughter. Another daughter (Pam) and her young family, including a six-year-old son, Dakota, lived a short walk away in a trailer. This daughter held things together as well as she could, with the help of hospice support. I don't know what would have happened to father and dying daughter otherwise.

Leonard (father) was a chain-smoker and drinker, severely depressed and resistant to treatment. Whenever I visited Janine (our patient), he would sit at the kitchen table, smoking constantly, just feet away from where his daughter always sat on a tattered recliner, tucked into place by a card table that held her play things. The seating arrangement reminded me of a baby's play station, one that keeps the child secure while giving her a surface to work on. Seeing a 43-year-old woman tethered like this was disturbing, but it was the one practical way for her caregiver sister, Pam, to keep her safe when she had to return to her own home and family.

The cabin was dark, dirty, crowded with stuff. The air and everything within was putrid with old cigarette smoke. At times during the winter, there was no running water or enough heat. Christmas decorations were left hanging throughout the year, either a sad attempt at cheer for a woman-child who had no clue what month it was, or forgetful laziness on the part of Dad who once said to me, "I'm just waiting for the next shoe to drop." I had seen lots of poverty during my musical excursions, but this was the worst. I had to learn how to set realistic priorities here. Dad was lost. Caregiver sister, although stressed and struggling, was a tough woman and would be OK. But Janine needed extra attention and lightness before she died. I could give her that. The big surprise here would be my growing friendship with young Dakota, who always showed up after school for Aunt Janine's music sessions. He alone personified hope and possibility in this dismal situation, and helped keep *me* afloat.

This family had a French/Indian ancestry, like mine. My Indian name highlighted our connection easily, and Pam, Dakota, even Dad, spoke proudly of their Indian blood. Shortly after Dakota's birth, he had been given his first Indian name, Little Talking Tree. He was, indeed, a bright and talkative child, curious about new things, and always wanting to take part. He loved his Aunt Janine very much, calling her "the baby" of the family, as everyone doted on her as such. Because Janine loved a visual connection to music, I often brought my medicine drum to play. A small glockenspiel, portable keyboard, shakers and bells were sometimes added to the mix. Both she and Little Talking Tree adored these musical toys, and music sessions were often more like childlike "orchestra" fests.

Janine's favorite song was "Kum Ba Ya" (a linguistic alteration of "Come By Here"). She was able to follow the song as I sang it, and join in with her own simplified version. At the start of each meeting, she would call from her chair, "Come sit here!", an echo of the words to her song. And at each session's end, she would say, "Where you goin'?" and "You are my friend!" Otherwise, our verbal communication was rare and very simple. It was when Janine *sang* that she communicated her feelings through facial expression, body movement, variation in tempo and tone. Her simple music was her way of making herself known to her little world, and to me.

I worked with this family for two years, such was the very gradual physical decline from uterine cancer that Janine had to live through. Despite the challenge of having to deal with an unsavory physical environment, I was grateful that we had a long time together. About a year into our work, sister Pam began taking Little Talking Tree to Abenaki drum circle gatherings. The Indian elders invited him to play the drum, taught him chants, and introduced him to the teachings of the Medicine Wheel and the Great Spirit. He started to bring what he was learning to our music sessions with Aunt Janine, very excited to teach me chants and drum beats. One day, he and his mother proudly announced that he had been given a new Indian name by the elders, one that he would grow into: White Thunder. From that day on, I addressed him properly, and continued to watch him grow.

As time passed, Janine's final decline set in. She was now being cared for as she slept on a mattress on the floor. The whole family was already mourning the loss of "the baby." One day, as I arrived for one of my final visits, I found White Thunder outside the cabin, standing on the edge of a deep ravine which opened onto a broad valley of thick forest. He was chanting, in full voice, "Wichita, doo ya, doo ya, doo ya, Wichita, heya, heya, heya"—and beating his drum with vigorous strength. He was only eight years old, but was tapping into the spirit of the man that he would become. His Aunt Janine lay dying inside, and White Thunder was grieving in his own way. I invited him to come in with me, but on this day, he preferred to stay outside. We decided together to give Janine her Indian name, so she would have it when she crossed into the spirit world. He chose Singing Flower. I heartily agreed, and assured him I would pass it on to her from him. I hugged him warmly, thanked him for all his help these many moons, and turned to go into the cabin to minister to Singing Flower. As I walked away, this little wise boy called out to me, "Runningdeer! It's the Circle of Life." Indeed, my young friend and teacher, it is.

Nine

The Will to Live,
The Will to Die

"What keeps us alive, what allows us to endure?
I think it is the hope of loving,
or being loved."

Meister Eckhart (Daniel Ladinsky, 2002)

I have long had a hunch that we human beings are powerful beyond measure, or at least that we have the potential to be so. When I was a very young woman, just embarking on a lifelong spiritual quest, I experienced a revelation of sorts: that somehow we could psychically will our own deaths. Now at first glance you may think this was simply fastastical, magical thinking on my part. But now that I have had the experience of 64 years of living, I am convinced that not only can we will our own deaths, but also our own lives.

As an artist, I have long experimented with the creative process, the way in which vision is imagined, incubated subconsciously, acted upon, and then manifested. I have used this process not only for artistic purposes, but as a way to conduct my life. With lots of repeated practice, I've become pretty masterful at this. I don't know if I could indeed will my own death, when the time comes for that. What I do know is that my will, or my intentionality, infused with a great trust in the forces of the universe to help me along, has actualized many wonderful outcomes in my life.

Rollo May, the American existential psychologist, wrote at length about human will:

> Intention is a conscious, psychological state; I can set myself voluntarily to do this or that. *Intentionality*, rather, refers to a state of being, and involves to a greater or lesser degree the totality of the person's orientation to the world at that time... The act and experience of consciousness itself is...a continuous molding and remolding of our world... Intentionality, as I am using it, goes below levels of immediate awareness, and includes spontaneous, bodily elements and other dimensions which are usually called "unconscious."

May's thinking and mine converge when he writes about "...a dimension of *trans*-consciousness...our way of discovering structure in the universe which our personal meanings reflect...a consciousness which reaches before, *ahead* of itself—in discovering new structures in reality, new laws, new forms..." [my italics] (May, 1965, pp.202–4, 209). He points toward a very powerful, creative impulse within each of us to effect change in our realities. We artists do this all the time, while making something new. But I have also witnessed the power of intentionality lead to some surprising and very unusual events in the dying processes of a number of people in my work and personal life.

My mother, Doris, died a year ago. She was 85 years old and had been ill with several co-morbidities, congestive heart failure, emphysema and kidney disease, for a long time. She had health challenges throughout her life. As a girl she was often sickened by a chronic and serious case of eczema. After birthing five children, and eventually raising them on her own, she developed Crohn's disease and lived with its difficult symptoms for many years. Finally, after more than 40 years of taking strong medications to help control the Crohn's, my mother's kidneys began to fail. She was in her late seventies by that time, and agreed to dialysis treatment, so she could continue living. She lived 85 years, the last seven of which were spent tethered to a dialysis machine, four hours per treatment, three or four treatments per week.

To introduce you to my mother, I'll just say she decided to perceive the long years of dialysis treatment as a late-life part-time job. She was funny. Doris had a challenging but very rich life. She was a stubborn Capricorn, loyal and loving to her family. She had a very interesting and effective way of shielding her eyes from things that were just too painfully hard to gaze upon, and rather focusing upon what needed to be done to get through the difficulty. She was a real pragmatist. But she was also an extremely spiritual and wise woman. She prayed often for many people, and cared for the sick and elderly during a long nursing career. The heart of her life was her family of grown children, grandchildren and great-grandchildren, all of whom adored her. She always maintained an optimistic (but not unrealistic) attitude about her life, no matter what was thrown in her path. She had a lot of psychic power. My mother was a wonderful woman, with a highly evolved soul.

Although Mom was never "my patient," we enjoyed a lifelong musical relationship. She was my earliest musical model. My best childhood memories are of falling asleep at night to the sounds of Mom playing her favorite piano classics, Broadway songs, light jazz and boogy-woogy. She was the one person in the world with whom I could listen quietly to a musical recording, savoring together all its beautiful nuances. She especially loved opera. Her eclectic musical taste served her well through thick and thin, always providing her with a special place for release and respite.

During the final years of her life, she lived with my brother and his family. She was happily secure in this warm home, and set her mind to maintaining a quality of life, right to the end, that was pretty good despite the necessity for lots of medical intervention. Although it became more and more difficult for her to continue on with dialysis treatments, she willingly took that burden on, so fervently did she wish to remain in the company of her large, loving extended family. She just didn't want to leave us.

Right up to the last week of her life, she cooked meals for my brother's family, sometimes hosted little luncheons for her surviving friends, took an online course in writing, and stayed in close contact with all of us, near and far. Her final year was especially daunting for her. She was losing weight and energy rapidly, had experienced several hospitalizations for breathing distress, and was finding it very difficult to keep up. My family knew that she would die soon, but given her refusal to stop dialysis treatment, it was unclear just how her death would go. We watched and waited.

Less than one week before she died, quite suddenly and quickly of a heart attack at home, she called her sister-in-law in Canada and admitted that she could no longer go on living. She was ready to let go and die. She chose not to tell me or my siblings, wanting to spare us from worry. In the few days that followed that decision to exercise her will and intentionality, she paid all her remaining bills, tidied up her bedroom, spoke to all her children (she called me just two hours before her death), and played her spinet piano for one last time. My brother remembers her playing an original song, written by my father, Gil Progen, who had left her decades ago. It's called "My Michelle," written for one of my sisters. As she played, she sang in a weak voice:

"A little pixie with a halo
who has a fairytale to tell
she makes the worries of the day go
that's My Michelle

She makes the sunshine seem much brighter
and makes the heart within me swell
all of my troubles seem much lighter
with My Michelle

While looking up at me
dressed in her fanciest clothes
I'm not surprised to see
that princess with mud on her nose
Her tiny head upon my shoulder
a sweetness that I know so well
so close to heaven when I hold her
that's My Michelle"

(Gil Progen, 1951)

My mother summoned the power of her stubborn, soulful nature when she willed herself to stay alive all those years, and then exercised that same willful intentionality when she finally decided to let go. I feel nothing but respect and a good measure of awe for the decisions she made, and the realities she was able to manifest.

It's important to note that published medical data states that a very high percentage of elderly people who receive dialysis to extend their lives die within two years of the onset of treatment. My mother shielded her eyes from that data, and lived well beyond that statistic. Her doctors considered her an anomaly. I believe it was her will that made it possible for her to live out many more satisfying years. And that it was her will, again, that set in motion a prompt and quick death. Brava, Doris!

I think the most unusual story I have to tell is of a four-day musical encounter I had with an 103-year-old woman named Alice. She was born in 1899, in late Victorian America, at a time when her hometown was a thriving destination for European immigrants looking for work in the great Rock of Ages granite quarry. At her unusually advanced age, she lived in a first floor apartment within one of the many gracious old Victorian homes that surround Currier Park. When these houses were built, those who profited most from the granite industry occupied them. Now they were as old as Alice herself, and many presented tired, paint-chipped facades while still suggesting the charm and propriety of their heyday. I noted the gingerbread trim on the gable and porch of her house as I approached her front door. The referring hospice nurse had instructed me to simply knock and enter. Alice was unable to rise and answer the door, and was expecting me.

"Come in, dear," she chirped softly as I entered her small parlor. Before me sat a delightful character from another era. Alice was tiny, very thin, with wrinkled translucent skin. She was dressed in a prim and pretty lace-trimmed dress, her thinning white hair combed neatly back on her small skull. Her eyes were blue and bright. She looked like a little bird perched on a branch, with nowhere to go. Her only concession to informality and comfort were the fluffy slippers on her feet and the hand-crocheted afghan on her lap. I sat on a crewel-covered stool so I could be a little lower than her level. It is a rare occasion that I am in the presence of such an aged elder.

I learned before our meeting that Alice had no apparent illnesses. She remained mentally very clear. She had enjoyed good health all her life, had raised children, grandchildren, great-grandchildren, and even lived to know her great-great-grandchildren. Her younger descendants stopped in every day, once in the morning and again in the evening after work, to check in on her. Her family had the good sense to ask her doctor for a referral to hospice services to provide her with the daily help she needed in order to stay in her home. But still, Alice spent most of her time alone, simply sitting on the sofa. Her family thought that music therapy might help her get through her long, lonely days.

Alice said she'd be pleased to have me sing for her. So I opened with a most fitting song, "Alice Blue Gown:"

> *"I once had a gown it was almost new*
> *oh the daintiest thing, it was sweet Alice Blue;*
> *with little forget-me-nots placed here and there,*
> *when I had it on I walked on the air,*
> *and it wore, and it wore, and it wore,*
> *till it went and it wasn't no more…"*

Joseph McCarthy and Harry Tierney wrote "Alice Blue Gown" in 1919, when Alice was just 20 years old. It referred to the favored color of Alice Roosevelt Longworth, daughter of Theodore Roosevelt. The song had its premier in the Broadway musical, *Irene,* and became a very popular tune of the day. The Alice who sat before me remembered it well from her youth, and was delighted to hear it sung again after so many, many years.

It has always impressed me how the simple, unselfconscious sharing of a song can so easily create an opening for intimacy and confidence between two people. Alice did not have a lot of energy to waste on conversation, so her utterances were very direct and to the point. No time for idle chatter. When I asked her how she spent her days, she replied, "I get up with the help of my aide, I get dressed and have just a few bites to eat. And then I am helped to this sofa, where I sit all day long, until I'm brought to bed." I wondered what she did during those hours. "Oh, I used to watch some television, but that doesn't interest me anymore. I no longer read or do my handwork. My eyes and hands are too old. I really don't have anything more to do here. I wonder..." I allowed Alice a few moments to sit quietly with what she told me, and then asked, "What do you wonder, Alice?"

"Do you think it would be alright if I decided to not get up anymore in the morning, to just stay in bed so I can die?" It seemed that she was asking me for permission to do something she was simply ready to do. Given her air of propriety and gentleness, I'm certain she did not want to do the wrong thing, to hurt her vast, extended family. While so many younger people who are facing end of life have such difficulty speaking about death, this very old lady had no trouble at all. I think I just managed to show up in her life at the right time, to listen and thoughtfully consider her very reasonable proposal. I answered her with no hesitation at all: "Alice, I think that's a marvelous idea. You have every right, after your long life, to rest in bed, to let go when you are ready. Your family will be fine. Would you like me to ask your aide to change your routine starting tomorrow?" "Why, yes, dear. That would be good!"

So Alice remained in bed the next morning, dressed in a soft, blue nightgown. I had noticed a picture of the ocean on her parlor wall the day we met, so I brought with me a few CDs of gentle music and ocean sounds when I visited late in the afternoon to see how the new plan was working out. When I arrived, Alice was asleep, wearing a look of peaceful relief on her ancient face. She never woke again—and died without any remarkable distress two days later.

Living a very long and healthy life can engender great clarity and power of will within a person, even within such a delicate, dainty personage as Alice. All she needed was a small nod of approval to enact her deepest wish and will: to finally bow to the forces of nature and end her work here on earth. No time was wasted, the decision was made. She simply got on with it, without a fuss.

We can thank both Doris and Alice for teaching us, through example, something about the powerful influence of mind upon the physical functions of the body. But what happens when there is little or no mind left to take part in the process of living and dying? If the seat of the will is the mind, what is left to tell the body what to do when that seat is diseased, diminished and on the road to disappearing?

I have seen too many cases of long, protracted dying among people with advanced stage Alzheimer's disease. These folks linger and linger among us, often bedridden, totally uninvolved with the world around them, while their loved ones watch the months and years pass by. It is a heartbreaking journey for all the players in this tragic drama. I've witnessed many a family member wish, perhaps even will, the passing of their loved one out of mercy, but with no actual result. Watching the enactment of these sad stories raises questions that have no easy answers; so little is yet known about the workings of a diseased brain. I wonder if there is any safe place left within the minds of those stricken for any shred of will or intentionality. If only we could do something to activate the will within such a patient, could the long, arduous process of dying be quickened, for the sake of ending suffering for all involved?

I do know that sharing the musical experience with Alzheimer's patients in all stages of the disease can lead to some remarkable results. Hearing music, especially live music presented directly to a patient, often interrupts the withdrawn, isolated mental state and redirects focus to the outer world. The music seems to wake people up from a lonely "slumber." It catalyzes a shift within the listener; they are *moved*. Those who cannot speak can often sing, enunciating words very clearly to songs they still remember. Sometimes these folks rediscover, at least for a moment, the ability to convey simple, meaningful verbal messages: "I love you." Most striking was the case of a burly man of Russian descent, dancing and singing all around a large common room packed with other patients in wheelchairs. His daughter informed me that before the onset of Alzheimer's, he had been a dour, serious man, who had no interest in music whatsoever. One more unforgettable experience surfaces: of an old woman on her deathbed, a former ballet dancer and teacher. As I played ballet music by Tchaikovsky at her bedside, she lifted her arms into the air and "danced" once more. She had been sleeping and unresponsive, well on her way to taking her last breath.

What's going on here? It undoubtedly has to do with the brain, and the mind. And the way music continues to have a powerful effect on both, despite neurological damage and the more comprehensive shutting down of the entire body as one dies.

Alzheimer's disease, simply stated, is the gradual killing of brain cells over a period of as little as two years to as long as 20, finally leading to death. Brain cells are damaged by the spread of plaques which are clumps of protein called beta-amyloid. This is also accompanied by the tangling of threads of tau protein which, in their normal state, carry needed nutrients to brain cells. Depending upon where these plaques and tangles are located, various brain functions are diminished and then destroyed. The disease process spreads at different paces and following different brain paths from one patient to the next. Given the many brain loci or control sites governing all the various physical, mental, emotional and perhaps spiritual functions of us humans, Alzheimer's lays siege to whatever crosses its path.

Several years ago I attended an international conference on music and the brain. I was one of only a few therapist types, surrounded by hundreds of neuroscientists from around the world. While I work within a holistic model, they study the effects of music on the brain from a much smaller, reductionist model. Despite our difference in approaches, I learned some important things from them. Musical apprehension takes place in a whole variety of different brain sites or loci. Different parts of the brain are activated, sometimes alone, sometimes in partnership with others, depending upon the musical activity. Simple music listening, singing, playing an instrument, all involve different constellations of brain site activity, sometimes sharing sites, sometimes adding or dropping off others. The brain also adapts to change, responding to the damage of some of its parts by strengthening parts that have been untouched by disease or injury. Scientists refer to this phenomenon as brain plasticity, which helps us understand why my Russian friend rather suddenly became musical as other functions were falling by the wayside.

It may seem that I've strayed a bit from my earlier question about the will. But here's the connection: if music can stimulate a person with Alzheimer's to speak, to wake up, to sing, to dance, to engage emotionally, to be *moved*, might it also have the ability to stimulate the will? The late Nobel laureate and scientist Francis Crick focused his later life studies on the connection between consciousness, free will and the brain. He, like Rollo May, hypothesized that willful decisions are made by both the conscious and unconscious mind working together (May's notion of a transconscious mind), and that the brain locus called anterior cingulate gyrus was likely the seat of the unconscious component of free will. I think it's interesting that this brain site also has to do with emotional utterances, maternal identification and separation anxiety. Crick also adds one more bit of colorful speculation: that neural circuits "reverberate" like musical strings reverberate, and that the sound value of 40 Hz (sound wave cycles per second; equivalent to a musical pitch somewhere between E and E flat) may be the neural frequency related to the experience of consciousness (Crick, 1994).

As Crick points out, the study of the brain is a very complex enterprise, and I will be the first to admit that my thinking on this subject is extremely elementary, indeed. But I do wonder if exposure to music might have some influence over the workings of this part of the brain, and whether or not the will to die might be somehow activated by the musical experience at the deathbed. If any neuroscientist out there reads this book, perhaps my simple thoughts will excite some future research in this fascinating direction. In the meantime, I shall continue to sing and play for the dying, in the hope of activating their will to let go, in peace.

Ten

Self-Care
Breathing Life into My Life

"Workers need poetry more than bread.
They need that their life should be a poem.
They need some light from eternity."

Simone Weil, 1952

More often than not, whenever I am asked what sort of work I do,
I get this response: a concerned look on the face, even a tiny gasp,
and then, "Wow! That must be a hard job, depressing." Sometimes
people just don't know what to say, but want me to say more. This
is such a perfect teaching moment for me. I am happy to go on and
let people know just how rich and satisfying this work is. And how
being around death and dying is *not* the scary, devastatingly sad or
depressing experience that one might expect.

Now, that's not to say that this work is easy. It's not. It takes a
lot of energy, sensitivity, skill and commitment. At times, situations
can be very sad. But that just enriches the experience. Another
typical response I sometimes hear is: "Oh, you must be a very special
person to do this!" Well maybe, but I think that assessment is a bit
overdone. It has taken years for me to attain a good measure of
ease and equanimity around end of life situations. Like any kind of
work, practice leads to maturity and excellence for the task at hand.
I have come to see death as the final stage of development in our

lives, and much like the midwife who ministers to the birth of a new biological life, I simply minister to the death of a body and the emergence of a soul.

When my editors asked me to write a chapter about self-care, I thought it would probably be brief, given my simple, common-sense approach to staying healthy. What I prescribe and describe here is necessarily custom-fit solely to me, my style, my personality. I expect that some things I do for myself may also work for others, while you will come up with other important practices that will suit you better than me. Nevertheless, there are a few basic needs that I believe anyone working in this field or any of the healing professions should pay attention to: the need for meaningful work, ample rest, plentiful play, loving personal relationships, healthy nutrition and adequate exercise, and daily doses of sensual beauty. The ways in which we fulfill these needs will be unique to who we are. Perhaps if I share with you how *I* go about living a healthier life, one that enables me to do particularly sensitive work with relative ease, it will help you to find your own solutions.

I have never been happy in a conventional nine to five job, though I've held several in my lifetime. Meaningful and happy work for me includes the use of my creativity, the ability to make a lot of my own decisions, a flexible time schedule, and the knowledge that I am making some positive difference in the lives of the people I work with. The years I taught piano and voice privately in my own studio, employing a pedagogical approach which included inner therapeutic work with my students, were very satisfying. That experience eventually led to my musical work in home hospice care, and now in a hospital setting. I have never done therapeutic work on a full-time basis, knowing that my constitution would not weather that kind of demand on physical, emotional and mental energy. I have never worked more than 24 hours per week in this field, and these days, even less. I have never expected anything more than a modest but fair income from my labors, recognizing that the balance of time available in my life for other important things is worth just as much as money. At the same time, it has taken me years to convince the powers that be that my hourly work is worth a good deal more than I ever made in a more conventional job. Because I am finally paid on a par with other medical professionals, I am able to work on a part-time basis, and still meet my modest needs. This gives me the energy to do high-quality work, not necessarily high-quantity work. Offering people a specialized kind of support at such a critical time in life fills my need to do work that makes a positive difference. My job allows me to use my musical and healing talents to help people become more at ease with life's final stage, to experience the process in a deeper way. An alternative artistic route, should I have pursued a stage performance career, would not have allowed me to tap into my innate strengths to guide and heal. This job fits me perfectly, and I never feel sluggish about going to work. The work I do, the human connections I make along the way, enrich my own life. The Dalai Lama talks about a special kind of happiness which is "an enduring comfort that results from the thorough transformation and development of the mind" (2012). I would add, "and the heart." Meaningful work such as this brings me that kind of happiness.

My need for rest is met in numerous ways. I look forward to sleep every night. I usually wake early and climb into bed by 10 p.m., if not earlier. Some people may view sleep as a waste of time, but I enjoy it as just a deeper form of consciousness in my day. While the body replenishes its energy, my mind has an opportunity to travel the dreamworld, often a place of sorting things out or feeding creative thought. But one does not need to be asleep to rest. I have practiced deep breathing for close to 40 years now, until it has become a habitual, unconscious body mechanism. I imagine the capacity of my lungs has strengthened over time, simply from more fully inflating and emptying them on a regular basis. This being the normal way that I breathe, my body does not easily fall into the stress response. When it does, as a result of something sudden and very alarming, it recovers quickly and easily. Living with high stress levels is very tiring, so I enjoy a more constantly restful state most of the time. Anyone can learn this. It takes time and practice, but the health rewards are great and lasting. I am particularly conscious of my breathing while working with patients and families. The more restful, calm energy I bring to the situation has a palliative effect on those present, helping to lower the general stress levels that are often heightened in end of life situations.

It happens that I now live alone, after six decades of always living with others. Although all the responsibility of maintaining my home is on me, which requires a good deal of physical work, I find the peace and quiet of not having to relate to others while at home very restful. If I talk to anyone, it's to myself or to the cat. And if I wish to be silent for hours on end, there's little to interrupt that. My home is in the country, a beautiful natural environment that lends itself to slowing down, with plenty of space and time to think and dream. Though carrying wood for the stove and doing yard work, shoveling the paths after a snowstorm and doing maintenance on the house require a good deal of physical energy and time, rural living feels much more restful to me than a noisy, fast, urban lifestyle. Just being able to sit outside in my garden to watch the sun set beyond the green meadow that is my backyard is a source of great peace and rest.

How do I play? This will be fun to answer! I used to be much more serious, even somber, in my youth. The oldest child of five, my childhood was far from carefree. My father's alcoholism and parents' divorce made for a pretty dark world for me, my siblings and my mother. What a long struggle it has been to rise above that time, to finally be able to let go of the compensating need to prove my worth, to accept my weaknesses with laughter, to simply relax with who I am. But I've done that, and the play that I missed out on during childhood is now abundant in my later years. I am delighted by the world! I finally feel a trust in the universe that allows me to take risks, to make mistakes, to reach for lofty success, to sometimes be the goofy and playful person that balances out the serious, exceedingly earnest me.

A very wise teacher of playfulness was delivered to me five years ago in the form of my beloved granddaughter, Olivia True. We have spent every Wednesday together since her birth. Doing my part to help raise her has been another kind of very meaningful work for me, which my flexible hospice and hospital schedules have allowed. But beyond the work of caregiving, Wednesday is a day of PLAY! Livee is full of energy, spunk and imagination. She is a much loved and happy child who knows how to have fun while learning about the world. I let her decide pretty much how we will spend our time together, and she never runs out of great ideas.

Together, we play dress-up with a great collection of fancy scarves and hats, old vintage slips and prom gowns. Sometimes we make cat tails out of crepe paper streamers, pin them to our behinds, and crawl around the house like frisky cats. We play Livee's version of Parcheesi (a board game), not following any of the game rules. We swing under the apple tree. We play ball outside, run around a lot, collect milkweed pods, follow the butterflies, pick the wildflowers, hike to the wetland and listen to the frogs. I play the piano while Livee dances. She plays the piano while I dance. We paint pictures out on the picnic table, make little balls out of sculpy dough and roll them on the floor. We bake cupcakes and gingersnaps. We sing and laugh, and then cuddle together in the big bed for a long nap. What joy!

When she is not around, I remember how to play in my own way. In the summer months I love to swim in the village pond, just down the hill from my house. I play music for myself, on my fine grand piano. I enjoy reading novels and watching rented films, while relaxing in an easy chair under a cozy afghan. Warm bubble baths in candlelight are a luxurious kind of play. Walking and gardening, though strenuous physical activities, feel like playful pursuits to me. Listening to the weekly live Boston Symphony Orchestra concert on public radio while stretched out on the sofa is a great pleasure, another kind of playtime.

I believe that when we enjoy ourselves, we fill up with a happy kind of energy that renews us, that makes it possible for us to continue to work and learn and grow. Play helps us feel closer to the people we play with, and brings us ever closer to our own true, loving, childlike natures. I will forever be indebted to little Livee for showing me just how to do it, with great joy and abandon.

Despite living alone, I enjoy many loving relationships. My daughter and granddaughter live nearby, so I spend regular time with both of them. They are my mainstay. My siblings and their families are scattered throughout New England and beyond, but I speak with them often, visit when I can, stay in touch with the young ones on Facebook. I can count many people as my friends, though social time with them is at a minimum. We are all busy, many of us in the healing professions. Although my relationships with patients and families are fleeting, I consider those to be loving as well. Connecting with people intimately, even briefly, is a source of great emotional nourishment for me. Through family, friends and work I counteract any feeling of isolation I might harbor as a result of living alone. And then there's my dear black cat, Patience. She is the living, breathing, warm creature that greets me at the door, snuggles with me at night, entertains me with her antics, argues with me when we don't see eye to eye. I am not alone in the world, and feel secure that as long as I continue to nourish my loving relationships, with time and attention and initiative, help and comfort will be there for me when I need it.

The most basic nourishment, food, is more of a challenge for me. I enjoy flavorful food very much. It is one of my favorite earthly pleasures. I also like to cook, not necessarily every day, but enough to fulfill my need for that kind of creative expression. I eat healthy, fresh foods from a constellation of food types. I have never, and probably never will, subscribe to any extreme diets. Giving up pasta or occasional sweets is totally against my nature, so I just eat them in moderation. As I age, my helpings have become smaller. I tend to eat when I'm hungry, not necessarily on a strict time schedule. A fair amount of food, organic vegetables and fruits, comes from my own garden and freezer. So I both save money and eat food that I know has not been chemically altered, fertilized or preserved. I don't see any reason to eat food that I don't enjoy. Taking care of ourselves should be relatively easy and pleasing, so we'll continue to do it over the long haul. The same goes for physical exercise. I am not a gym rat. Exercise machines bore me, the loud pounding music at the gym gives me a headache. So I walk a half mile down the hill to the pond and back up to my house several times a week, sometimes less in wintry weather. I studied dance when I was younger and still enjoy stretching on my carpet. When Livee visits, I go non-stop. And when I clean my house or weed the gardens, I stretch and lift, raise my heartbeat and work up a sweat. These are common-sense approaches to exercise that correlate with my lifestyle and the activities that I like to do. At 64, I continue to look younger than my years, and although I suffer the aches and pains of many a sexagenarian, my body still functions pretty well. I would encourage anyone to simply maintain a reasonable, moderate approach to healthy living, and you should do just fine.

Fortunately, I live in a beautiful rural state where I am almost always surrounded by nature's beauty. I notice it all each day, and take in the visual richness like a medicine. Living in a northerly clime, color and light are very important ingredients to staying vibrant and above depression during the long, grey months of the Vermont winter and spring. I love decorating my home environment where color and light are used liberally and adventurously. My furniture is a mix of antiques, yard sale items and family heirlooms. Old things, art made by friends, rugs from other cultures, pottery, photos of current family and long-dead ancestors, every artifact holding its own meaning—these are what decorate my little haven. Both silence and sound are well provided, simply by turning on or off a good sound system that has served me for over 40 years. While sleeping out on the screen porch in summer, I can listen to the peepers in the nearby wetland as I fall asleep. And then of course the live sounds of piano, dulcimer, shruti box, ukelele, all instruments I play and use in my work, often fill the rooms of my cottage, and in good weather float through my windows out beyond into the garden. Adding a handful of cloves to the steampot on the woodstove makes the household air fragrant. Wrapping myself in a mohair shawl on a late autumn evening while waiting for the fire to catch nourishes the tactile sense, as do clean crisp bedsheets that have been hung out on a line to dry in the sunny breeze.

These may be aspects of living that you may not consider to be crucial to well-being. If you haven't taken the need for sensual beauty into account, you might begin slowly, by making one simple change, and then another. Light a candle on the table when your family shares a dinner. Instead of purchasing another pair of shoes that you really don't need, look for a painting or print that stirs your imagination and make it a gift to yourself. Move the furniture around, create a bit more spaciousness in a room that you spend a lot of time in. You will come to notice that manipulating your home environment in these simple ways can lift your mood, help you feel more calm, and instill within you more gratitude and appreciation for small things. The best way to offset the ugliness that pervades our world is to create more and more beauty. And our homes are a good place to start.

I did not mention spirituality in my introduction to this chapter on self-care, mostly because not everyone has a spiritual component in their lives. But I must include it here as one of the most important aspects of my own self-care. I am not religiously affiliated in any way, to any church or temple or practice. But my life is infused with spirit, and I have created a way of including my own brand of spiritual practice into my daily life as a strong reminder that I do not live, work, play, love or enjoy as a separate entity in this world.

I believe that I am a very small part of something very big and mysterious. That I am connected to all living things by filaments of energy, and that because of that, we can influence each other's states of being. That there are forces for good and evil all around us, and that I have an opportunity, as well as a responsibility, to choose which forces I wish to engage with, to amplify. I feel that I do not work alone, that simply by asking for help from spiritual allies, I can work in collaboration with some pretty powerful sources of energy while I stand on this earth. I don't really know what God is, but I name this magnificent source of all beingness the Great Spirit. In various places within my home are symbols that remind me of this mysterious presence. Whenever I walk through the doors of the hospital where I work, I sometimes imagine a big hawk flying at my side, and I ask for guidance and strength in preparation for the work that's ahead of me. I pray often for the people in my life, "surrounding them, and myself, with radiant light, love and truth," a spiritual mantra taught to me by my mother. And finally, I give great thanks: for the special gifts I've been given, my enduring health, the loving people in my life, the opportunity to help others, and the unwavering spiritual presence that watches over it all.

We cannot care for others in the very best way unless we have cared for ourselves first. The quality of healing energy we offer those in our charge depends on how consistently we nourish healthy energies within ourselves. There is no way around this. I am reminded of a simple daily mantra, shared with me by my sister: "Be happy, be healthy, be free!" Cultivate this way of being, and your life and work will be a blessing to others.

Eleven

Colophon
Lessons and Final Thoughts

"There is in God, some say,
a deep but dazzling darkness…"

Henry Vaughan, 17th-century Welsh poet
("The Night," Poetry Foundation, 2012)

I have walked very close to the edge of life's precipice with hundreds of dying people. I've often thought it strange that I've been present at the actual moment of death with only two people that I can recall. After all, it's but a moment in time, albeit a dramatic and very meaningful one. I've learned that to predict the time of death is a futile effort, so capricious and complex are the many interactions between body, mind and spirit that constitute the process of dying. For a hospice worker, being present at the time of death is a simple gift, an experience that is unforgettable.

The two deaths I witnessed were about as different as one could imagine. They were like bookends on opposite sides of a spectrum of relative ease and distress while dying. The first was so peaceful and unexpected I wondered for several minutes if it had actually happened. I had just arrived for a first meeting with an elderly woman who I knew was nearing death. She lay asleep on a cot in the open room of her trailer. Her adult daughter and daughter-in-law were busy in the kitchen defrosting her old refrigerator by hand, scraping the stubborn ice of the freezer away with small hammers and chisels. The two women were talking amiably as they worked. It was about as ordinary a scene on the old farmstead as could be imagined, the younger generation watching over the elder as the day's work was being done. With little fuss I sat in the chair next to the sleeping woman, opened my songbook and said: "Tilly, my name is Islene. I'm a music therapist with the hospice team, and I'd like to sing for you while you rest. I hope that's OK." Before I had a chance to open my mouth and sing the first note, Tilly took one more breath, exhaled, and then became very quiet. I waited for the next breath to begin before singing, but it never came. I sat quietly and waited a full three minutes before I touched Tilly's head in blessing and then slowly walked over to the refrigerator to tell her daughters that I believed she had just died. What a beautifully peaceful way to go. And what a stroke of good luck for me that my first moment of death experience was so gentle.

The next time I walked into a moment of death, several years later, was agonizing. It was with a woman with whom I had worked for a short time in a nursing home. She was anxious, alone, afraid of dying, and intractable in her position. She had a history of mental illness. Though our music sessions brought some temporary relief, the abiding fear of death always returned with its fierce grip. I arrived one morning to find a nurse and two aides struggling to turn her body in bed to relieve her pressure ulcers. Patient Agatha was kicking her legs, digging her heels into the mattress, attempting to push her body up the wall, all the while screaming and moaning in desperate fright. It looked as if she were fighting to get out of her own skin. At last, the aides were able to place her body back onto the bed, as she took her last terrible breath. No musical notes were sung that day either. Instead I did my best to comfort the nurse and aides. We had all just witnessed a very traumatic event, a terrible death.

The image of the precipice presents us with different perceptual possibilities. We can view it as the edge of a very high cliff from which we will fall and shatter. We can perceive it as the absolute end of existence, followed by nothingness. Or we can use it as a launching pad to flight. Poor Agatha expected to fall. Tilly took off like a glider. I prefer the latter perception to the former, myself. None of us will know for sure until we step off the edge of the precipice. Perhaps each of us will find what we expect: some will fall and crash, some will vanish, others will soar. I cannot be certain about these things. Most likely, something I cannot even begin to imagine will occur. Like many of us, I simply hope, hypothesize and wonder. And sometimes I wish that a few of my deceased patients would drop me a hint in my dreams.

Despite my lack of hard knowledge about any of this, I still feel a strong sense of continuum. One of the questions I am left with after doing this work for more than a dozen years now is: is any life ever truly finished? My nature is optimistic, and I believe in our deeply creative ability to define and design our own realities. Life feels like one long succession of creative acts to me, and I have no reason to believe that this essential creative energy will not continue on after the physical body dies. It's basic Einsteinian law: energy is infinite. So, perhaps we go on in some rarefied form. Hindus and Buddhists understand this phenomenon as reincarnation. People the world over have been asking these same questions for centuries, applying their own understandings to the way they live and die. I think reincarnation, like many traditional beliefs, is a very interesting and plausible concept. But I also believe that this creative essence within us doesn't necessarily need a physical body to do its work. At this point in such lofty musings, my goofy self is laughing at my exceedingly earnest self, thinking: "Blah, blah, blah... I'm just *so* curious, I almost can't wait to find out!" But of course I'll wait. I'm not ready to die yet. There's still too much to do and learn.

As I think about past patients, it would be hard to believe that any of them did not still have plans and wishes for a future. And probably still many things left undone. My own mother deeply desired to be able to stick around for more happy family occasions together. I remember chuckling when she said, just months before her death, "I really want to be around to see Olivia grow up and graduate." Olivia was four years old at the time, and Mom was clearly on her last leg. But despite her ever-weakening state, and the fact that she knew she was dying, Mom could still see a continuum ahead of her. I recall patients who had to leave important things undone. Those who never made good peace with close family members. Or finished an artistic work they were in the middle of. Or got to ride in a hot air balloon. Or were able to finish raising their children. Or finish building a house for their family. Or grew up from toddlerhood. Or grew old into wisdom or foolishness. I can think of only one past patient who didn't seem to have anything at all left to do on earth: 103-year-old Alice. But who knows what her plans may have been for the beyond! I wonder if Franz Schubert has finished his symphony in some netherworld!

Little snippets of stories bubble up in my memory as I consider these questions and lessons. I just woke at 2 a.m., remembering the afternoon I arrived at a home for a scheduled session to find that the dear woman had died just an hour earlier, as I was driving there. Her skittish family was hovered around the kitchen table drinking coffee, waiting for the undertaker to arrive, not wanting to get anywhere near the dead body which was safely hidden behind a closed bedroom door. I asked if I might sit with the deceased for them, and maybe sing, which was granted with some amount of relief and not a little surprise. I didn't mention that I felt the spiritual drama occurring in the next room called for a witness. They were spooked enough. So I went in and sang while their elder's body grew cold. Honoring the continuum.

Dying can even be funny. I recall the time a hospice nurse was attempting to put in place a urinary catheter for a patient who was still quite alert but no longer able to get up to use the commode. After two tries, with still no flow from a distressingly full bladder, I very spontaneously pressed the play button on the CD player, crossing my fingers that the music disc left inside might be appropriate. As the Baroque sounds filled the room, the patient exclaimed, "Oh! That's the music we swam to in my water ballet class at summer camp!" Before she finished the sentence, her water gushed through the tubing into the bedpan. We all laughed together, delighted by the image and how it "broke the dam." We laughed even louder when I told them the music we were listening to was Handel's *Water Music* suite!

Dying can be hard on people, especially family and friends. Caregiving at home or sitting a long death vigil in a hospital or nursing home is exhausting work. Family members often put their own needs aside at this time, foregoing sleep, food, fresh air and exercise. As I accompany the soloist making passage, my job is also to coach those around the dying, as if they are a chamber ensemble. Reminding people to eat and sleep is a simple way I can help. But there are deeper levels of need that must be tended to. Thomas Aquinas's words "beauty arrests motion" take on special meaning when I bring music to a bedside vigil. Music can help all *be* with the experiences of dying and loss. The beauty of music tends to stop the action, the chatter, the busy work that often serves as a safe diversion from what's really going on. People need to sit quietly, feel their feelings, remember the important things shared, and regenerate their energy so they can truly focus on loving and letting go. The thick defenses that rise up when we must confront the death of a loved one are often diluted when the beauty of music arrests motion. I have witnessed countless examples of tears shed, stories shared, thoughtful silence, honor and gratitude bestowed upon the dying as I've made music at the deathbed. This is true vigil: an alert watchfulness of a beloved's leave-taking, while we recognize and open to our own internal responses. Nearness to death gives us a perfect opportunity to learn more about ourselves and each other.

I've discovered that it's never too late to change something essential about our personal natures. I recently saw this happen when an old woman who had never been physically demonstrative of affection reached out and stroked the face of her caregiver, telling her she was the daughter she never had. I saw it in the eyes of a hospice nurse who was dying after a mid-life stroke. She was receiving care from our hospice team, of which she had been a long-time member. Despite the great support I received from my teammates for the special and unusual work I do, this nurse was always skeptical, not wanting me to get anywhere near her as she declined during her final months. When one evening all her colleagues arrived to celebrate and pamper her, I tucked my piano in the corner of the room and played "Amazing Grace," her favorite song. When the music registered in her consciousness, she turned her head and looked deeply into my eyes as I played for her. No words were needed to let me know that she had changed her mind.

I recall the final days of caring for my own father, as he died from lung cancer. He hated being taken care of, was a very proud and well-defended man. Our relationship through the years had not been easy, but I was determined to see him through his last days. One night he insisted on walking, with no help, to the bathroom so he could urinate. No bedpans or catheters for him! I pleaded with him to let me guide him as he walked, but he would have none of it. So I let him go. Standing just outside the closed bathroom door, I heart a thump and a moan. I found Dad lying helplessly on the tile floor, unable to move. As I approached to lift him up, he said, "No, no, I can do it." In that moment I took charge and replied, "Dad, you're a bag of bones, and we're going to do this together." He laughed sardonically, as if at a private joke, and echoed, "A bag of bones, a bag of bones." From then on, he let himself receive the loving help he had rejected much of his life.

And what have *I* learned from this amazing period in my life? I've learned as much about music as I have about death and dying. I sing with a deeper, freer, more resonant voice. I know more songs than I ever thought possible, even making a few Hank Williams hits my own (who would have thought country music would be in my repertoire?). At the piano I'm now able to take risks that would have frightened me years ago, leading to the most sensitive and sonorous playing of my life. The very difficult scores don't seem so hard anymore. Being so close to death so often and for so long has taught me how to trust, how to feel, how to connect, how to express, how to be—all the lessons any aspiring musician must face and devour if he or she is to get anywhere worthwhile. My music has grown with me. What started out as a simple joy in childhood has become my own best medicine and one of my life's richest treasures.

I've also learned that I am capable of much more than I ever expected to accomplish. I've learned that teamwork is essential to caring for the dying. That everyone I encounter, patient, family, medical staff, has something to teach me about living. I've learned when to pursue, when to let go. I accept the fact that my input and influence is often small and fleeting; and that seeds of healing will germinate where they can. I can acknowledge that I do this work well, in all humility. One becomes more honest, clearer about priorities, more securely exposed when one hangs out with death. I've learned that there is little time to waste with pretense, while paradoxically, people in my care should be granted as much time as they need to open up to what is happening within and around them. I've long believed that we have an infinity of time to do what we will, but in some situations, such as death and dying, the clock is ticking. I am charged with keeping my own vigil: to recognize those moments when opening and growth might be possible for anyone involved, to nurture that gently before the opportunity vanishes, as it will. Beautiful music allows me to buy a little time, as it slows down and arrests motion, delivering us all to a place of suspension and sometimes realization.

There's still much work to be done. If we as a society are to truly honor end of life and transition into death as the crowning developmental stage of each human being, we must talk about it more, teach about it more, offer more opportunities for people to experience death and dying in safe and well-supported places. More doctors need to be convinced that dying people are not evidence of their failure to heal. Young nurses need to be able to explore their own personal issues with dying, their own deaths and the deaths of people in their care. The general cultural fear of death can be quieted simply by bringing it out into the open. There's nothing like direct exposure to the fearful experience for putting things in more manageable, and much less threatening, perspective.

Palliative care must not be limited to pharmaceutical interventions for managing pain and other distressful symptoms, both physical and emotional. All hospice teams and palliative care departments in hospitals *must* include expressive therapists, such as music and art therapists, as well as massage therapists, Reiki practitioners, and spiritual counselors, if tending to the needs of the whole person is truly their mission. Doctors, nurses, social workers, and all the rest of us must work together like a well-tuned orchestra, to share the responsibility equally and be recognized fully for the importance of our individual contributions to the whole. We are certainly not there yet. But I believe it's possible, and even necessary, if humanity is to achieve a new and healthier relationship with death and dying.

Working toward eliminating fear of death may be the ultimate way to cure many ills of the world.

The novelist Michael Ondaatje has so beautifully written: "There is a story always ahead of you. Barely existing. Only gradually do you attach yourself to it and feel it. You discover the carapace that will contain and test your character. You find in this way the path of your life" (Ondaatje, 2011, p.181). I see more stories and lessons ahead of me. And when it is my time to die, I expect I will have to face the natural fear of extinction that rises within any animal. But I also expect that the things I've learned while accompanying others on this final path will help me to relax, trust, express my needs and my love, to forgive, to feel gratitude, to open myself to whatever comes next. That's what I hope for myself. And for all of us.

In parting, may I sing for you?

"May Your Soul Be Well"
(Islene Runningdeer, 2012)

References

Achterberg, J. (1985) *Imagery in Healing: Shamanism in Modern Medicine*. Boston, MA: Shambala Publications.

Adler, K. (1965) *The Art of Accompanying and Coaching*. New York, NY: Da Capo Press.

Banks-Smith, N. Available at www.brainyquote.com/quotes/authors/n/nancy_banks_smith.html, accessed 21 January 2013.

Bishop, H. and Payne, J. (1947) "Home, Sweet Home." *All American Song Book*. New York, NY: Robbins Music Corporation. (Original work published in 1823.)

Cankú Lúta. "The Echoes of Sand Creek." Available at www.canku-luta.org/fall00/sand_creek.html, accessed on 18 January 2013.

Coghill, A. and Mason, L. (1942) "Work for the Night is Coming." *All American Song Book*. New York, NY: Robbins Music Corporation. (Original work published in 1864.)

Collins, P. (1982) "Thru These Walls." New York, NY: EMI Publishing.

Cook, A.S. (1902) *Select Translations from Old English Poets*. Boston, MA: Ginn and Co.

Crick, F. (1994) *The Astonishing Hypothesis: The Scientific Search for the Soul*. New York, NY: Touchstone.

Curtis, N. (ed.) (1987) *The Indians' Book: Authentic Native American Legends, Lore and Music*. New York, NY: Bonanza Books.

Dalai Lama (2012) Facebook post. Available at www.facebook.com/?ref=tn_tnmn#!/DalaiLama, accessed 15 April 2013.

DuBois, C.G. and Kreber, A.L. (1908) "The religion of the Luiseño Indians of Southern California." *University of California Publication in American Archeology and Ethnology 8*, 3, 110.

Evans-Wentz, W.Y. (1960) *The Tibetan Book of the Dead*. New York, NY: Oxford University Press.

Finney, D. (ed.) "Native American Wisdom." Available at www.greatdreams.com/wisdom.htm#Aupumut, accessed 18 January 2013.

Gibbons, O. (1929) *Silver Swan*. Boston, MA: E.C. Schirmer Music Co.

Hall, D. (2002) "Distressed Haiku." *The Painted Bed*. Boston, MA: Houghton Mifflin.

Hawkins-Boyle, Rev. K. *Death and Dying from a Native American Spirituality Perspective*. Available at www.aclergyguidetoendoflifeissues.com/Portals/1777/CS%20Resources/CS%20Native%20American, accessed on 20 January 2012.

Henderson, A.C. (1991) *American Indian Poetry: An Anthology of Songs and Chant*. New York, NY: Ballantine Books.

Henri, R. (1960) *The Art Spirit*. Philadelphia, PA: Lippincott, Williams and Wilkins.

Hillman, J. (1996) *The Soul's Code: In Search of Character and Calling*. New York, NY: Warner Books.

Holy Bible, "Book of Job." King James version: 30:30–3.

Ladinsky, D. (trans.) (2002) *Love Poems from God: Twelve Sacred Voices from the East and West*. New York, NY: Penguin.

Langer, S. (1957) *Problems of Art*. New York, NY: Charles Scribner's Sons.

Lhalungpa, L. (trans.) (1977) *The Life of Milarepa*. New York, NY: E.P. Dutton.

May, R. (1965) "Intentionality: The heart of human will." *Journal of Humanistic Psychology* 5, 2, 202–9.

McCarthy, J. and Tierney, H. (1919) "Alice Blue Gown." Sheet music. New York, NY: Jerome Feist Inc.

Morissette, A. (1998) "Sympathetic Character." Los Angeles, CA: Universal Publishing Group.

Morissette, A. (1998) "That I Would Be Good." Los Angeles, CA: Universal Publishing Group.

Noddings, N. (2002) *Educating Moral People: A Caring Alternative to Character Education*. Williston, VT: Teachers College Press.

Ondaatje, M. (2011) *The Cat's Table*. New York, NY: Alfred Knopf.

Proctor, A. and Sullivan, A. (1937) "The Lost Chord." *Songs You Like to Sing*. Boston, MA: G. Schirmer. (Original work published 1858.)

Shakespeare, W. (c.1600) *The Tragedy of Hamlet, Prince of Denmark*, Act IV, Scene 3, p.128. In E. Hubler (1963) *Signet Classic*. New York: Penguin Group.

Schindler, M.D. (1841) "O Sing to Me of Heaven." *The Southern Harp*. Boston, MA: Parker and Ditson Publishers.

Vaughan, H., "The Night." Available at www.poetryfoundation.org/poem/180789 accessed on 23 January 2013.

Weil, S. (1952) *Gravity and Grace*. London: Routledge.

Wesley, C. (1807) "Funeral Hymn by the late Rev. George Whitefield" in *A Collection of Hymns and Psalms for the Use of Singing School and Musical Societies*, Husband, J. (ed.) Lancaster, PA. (Original work published 1790.)

Index